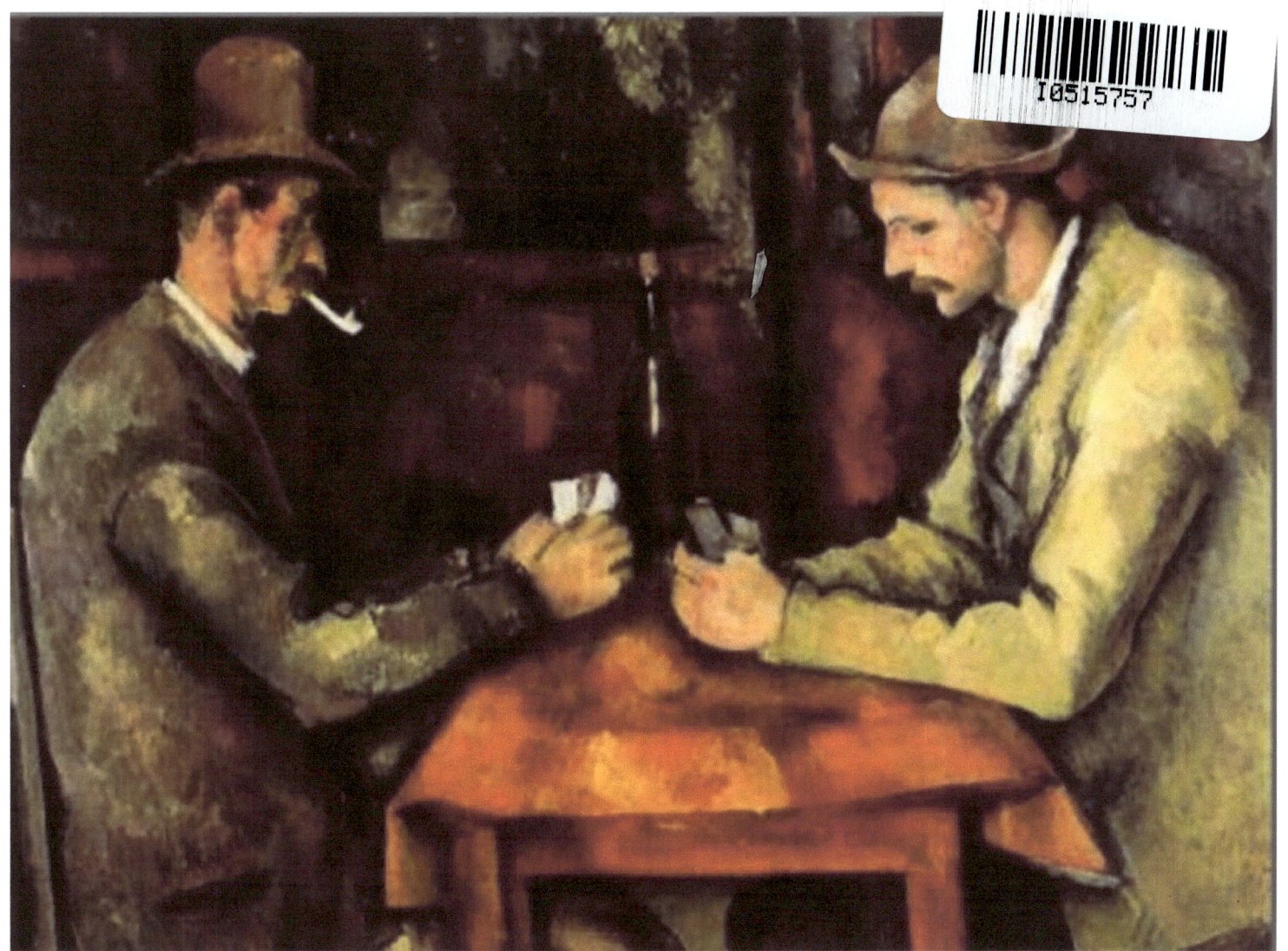

A Paul Cezanne, 1890s

The Card Players is a series of oil paintings by the French Post-Impressionist artist Paul Cezanne. Painted during Cezanne's final period in the early 1890s, there are five paintings in the series. The versions vary in size, thenumber of players, and the setting in which the game takes place. Each painting depicts Provengal peasants immersed in their pipes and playing cards. One version of The Card Players was sold in 2011 to the Royal Family of Qatar for a price estimated at between $250 million and $320 million,making it the third most expensive work of art ever sold.

WELCOME! We hope you will enjoy this Fave Art-17 photo album of my favorite random collection of art. Photos are copied from the internet, posters, calendars, cards and art books. You may display this book as coffee table book in your living room, as conversation piece. You may give this as gift. You may cut out each page, 8.5x11 inches, for framing. Printed by Tatay Jobo Elizes under following ISBN Code Numbers:

ISBN-13: 978- 1975796686 & ISBN-10: 1975796683

Printed in USA, 2017. Free to copy by anybody. Why copy? Just obtain the book.

Contact: job_elizes@yahoo.com (Tatay Jobo Elizes, Self-Publisher)

http://tinyurl.com/mj76ccq & http://www.jobelizes6.wix.com/mysite.

Fave Art - 17

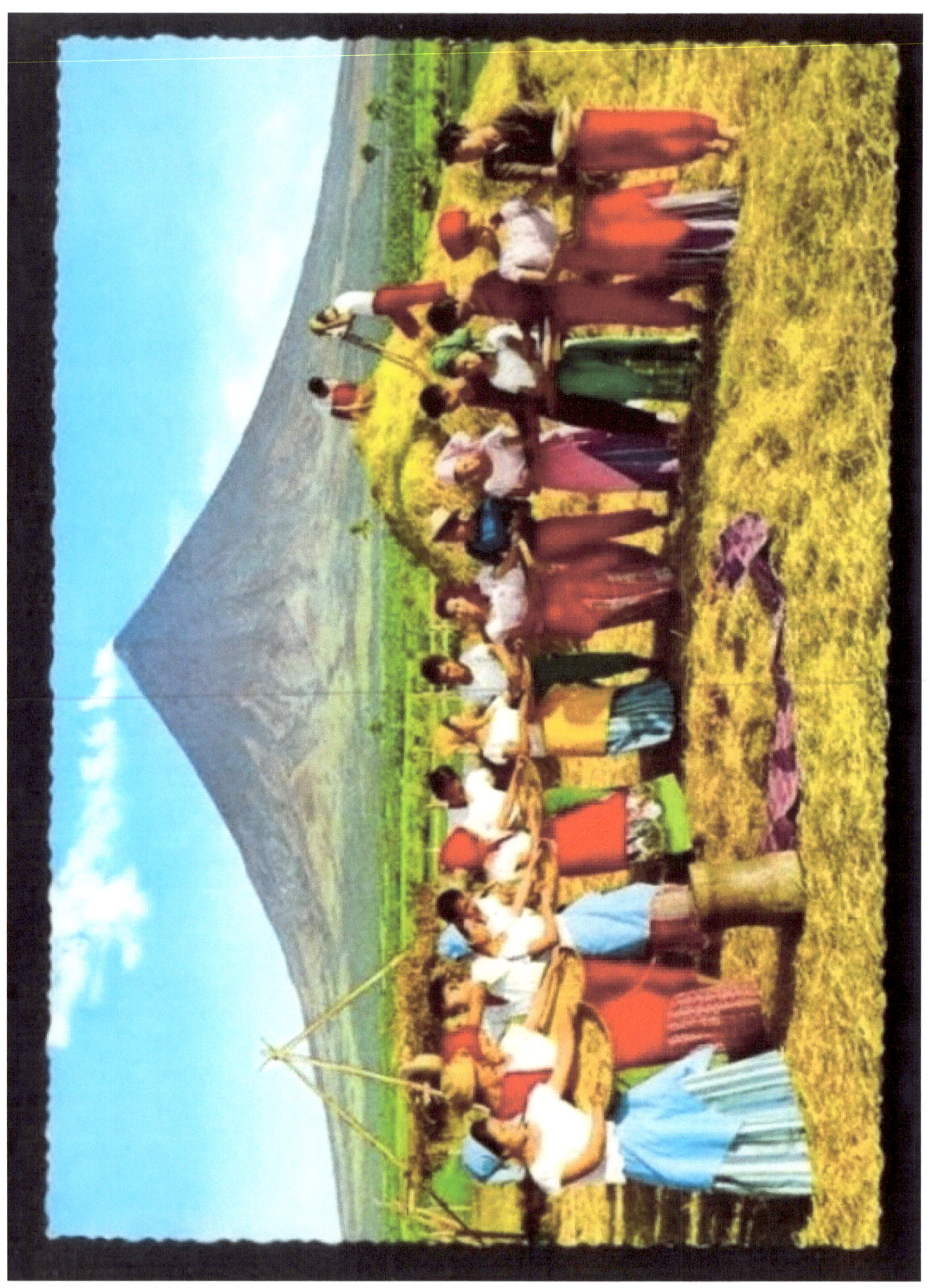

Mayon Volcano – A calendar Photo – Artist unknown

Fave Art - 17

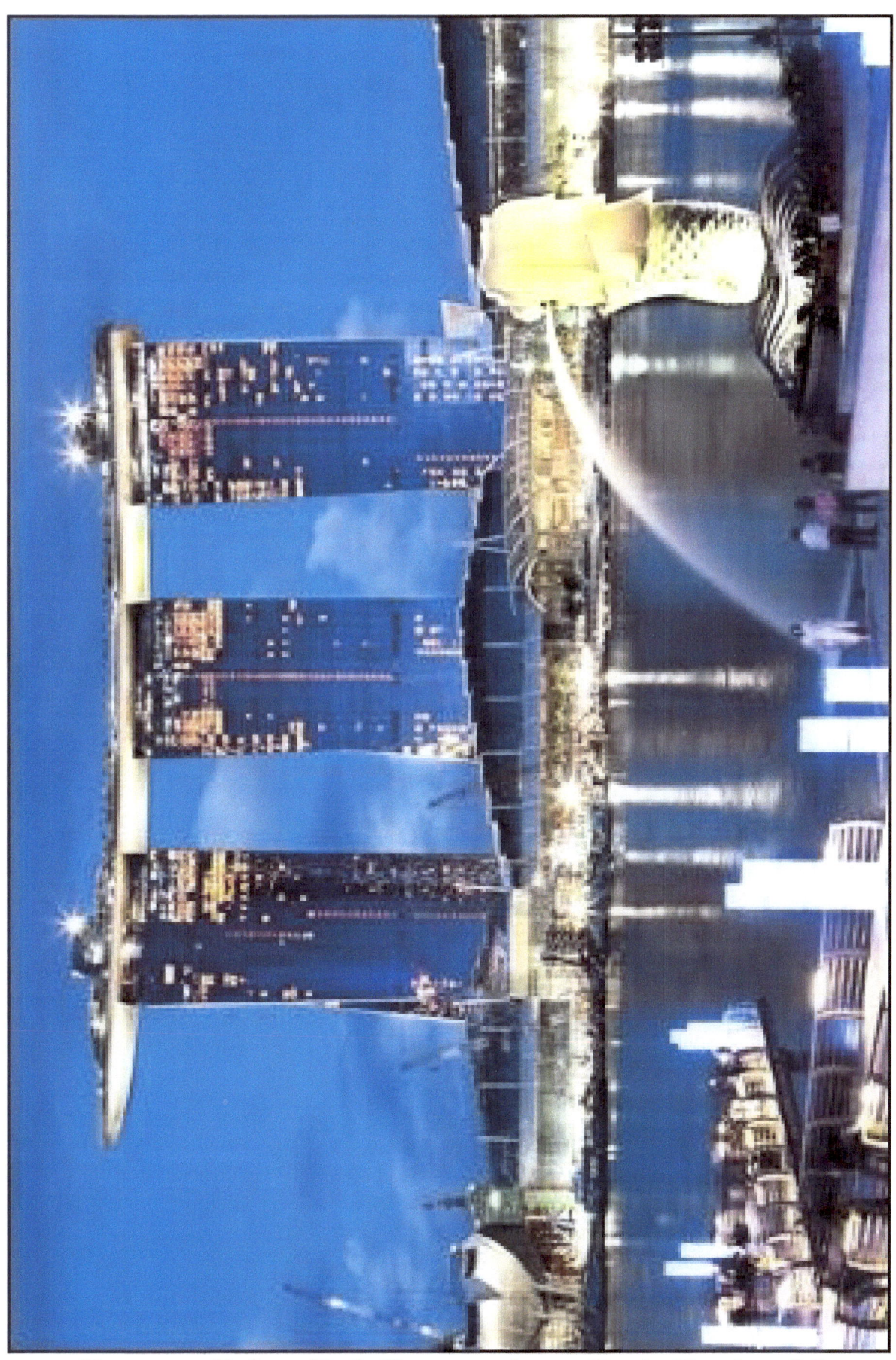

Singapore Unique Twin Towers + Large Boat – Tourism Ad

Fave Art - 17

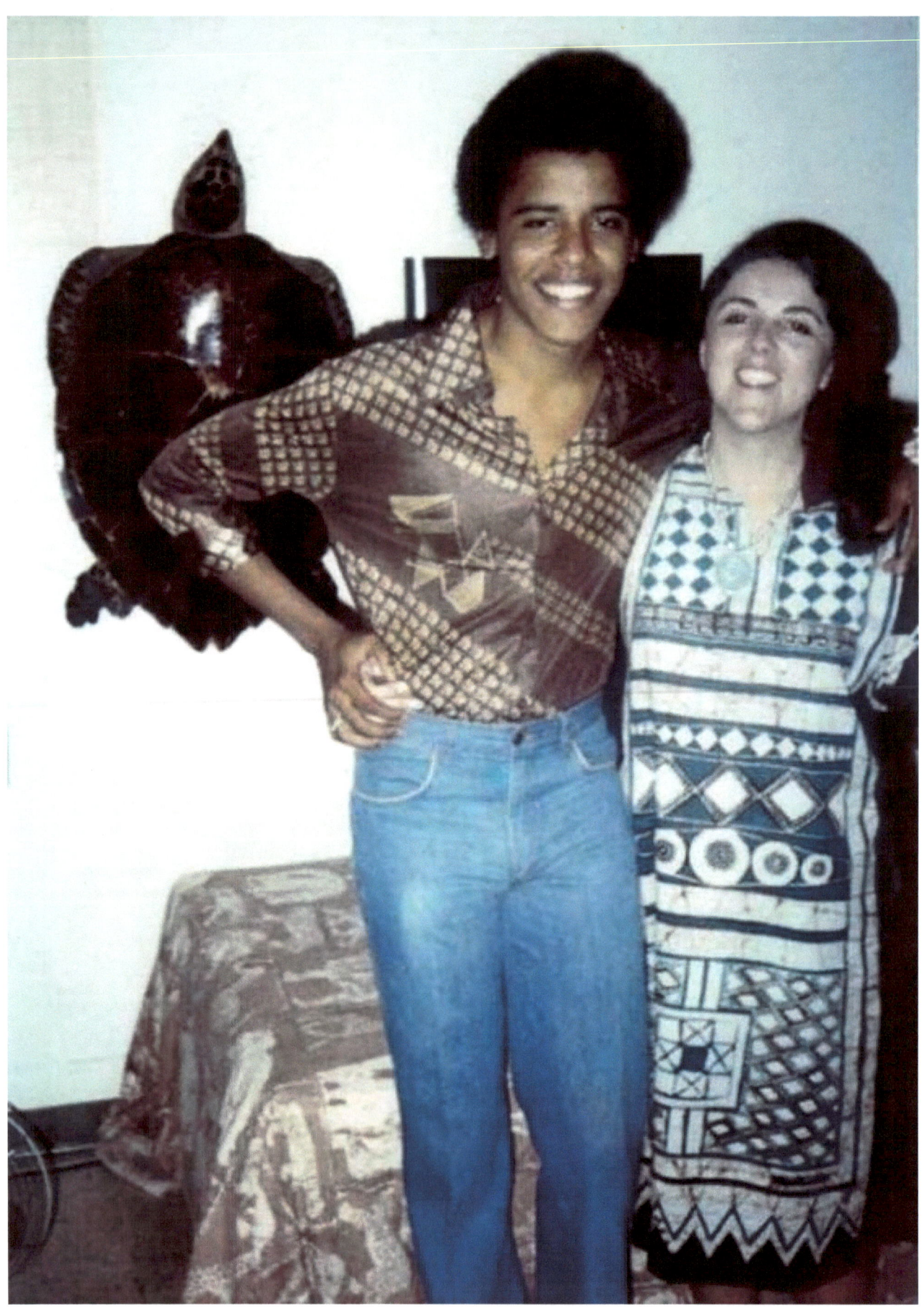

Young Barack Obama with his mom Ann Dunham – Unique Photo

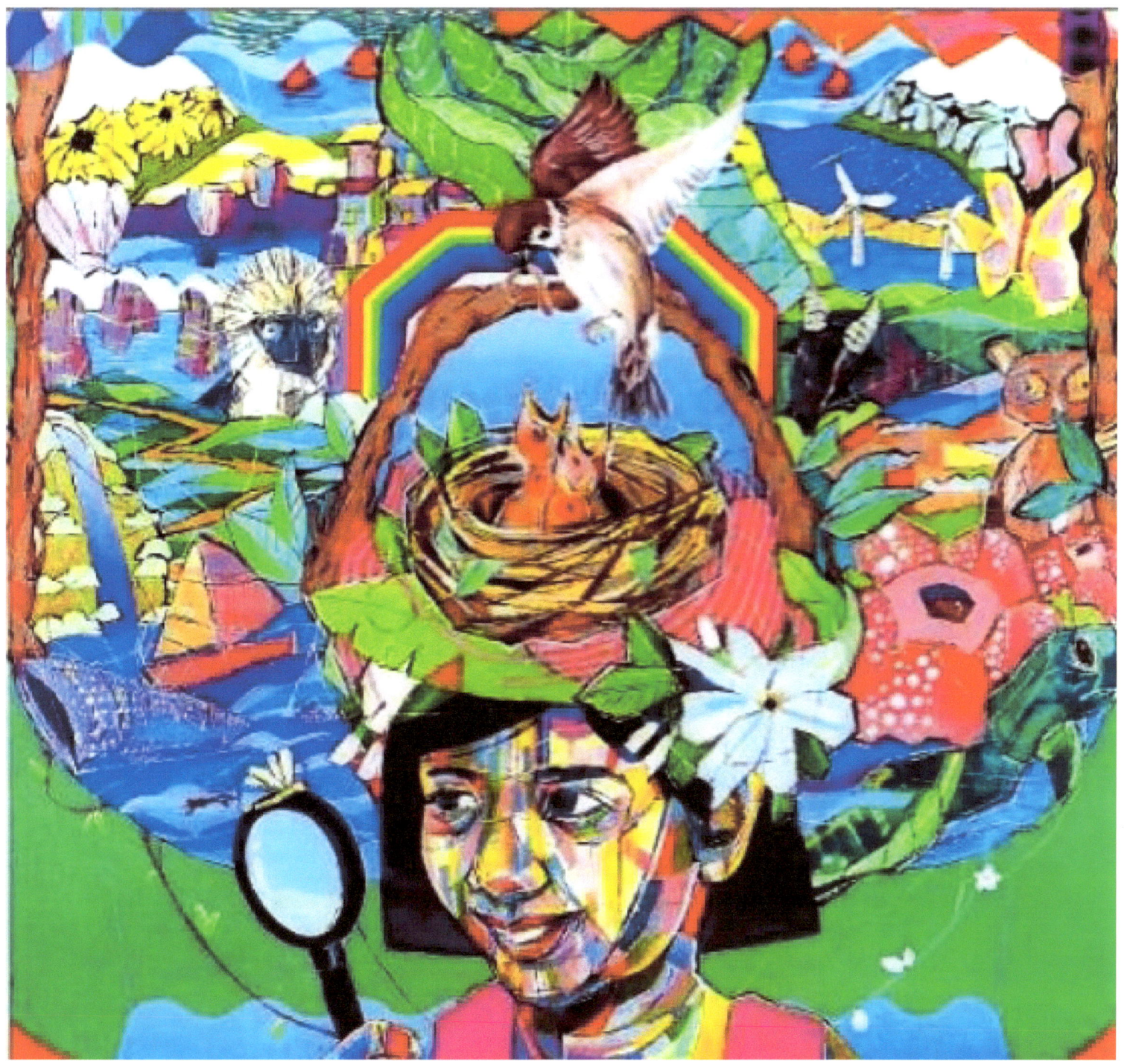

A Child's Imagination – Artist Unknown

WELCOME! We hope you will enjoy this Fave Art-17 photo album of my favorite random collection of art. Photos are copied from the internet, posters, calendars, cards and art books. You may display this book as coffee table book in your living room, as conversation piece. You may give this as gift. You may cut out each page, 8.5x11 inches, for framing. Printed by Tatay Jobo Elizes under following ISBN Code Numbers:

Fave Art - 17

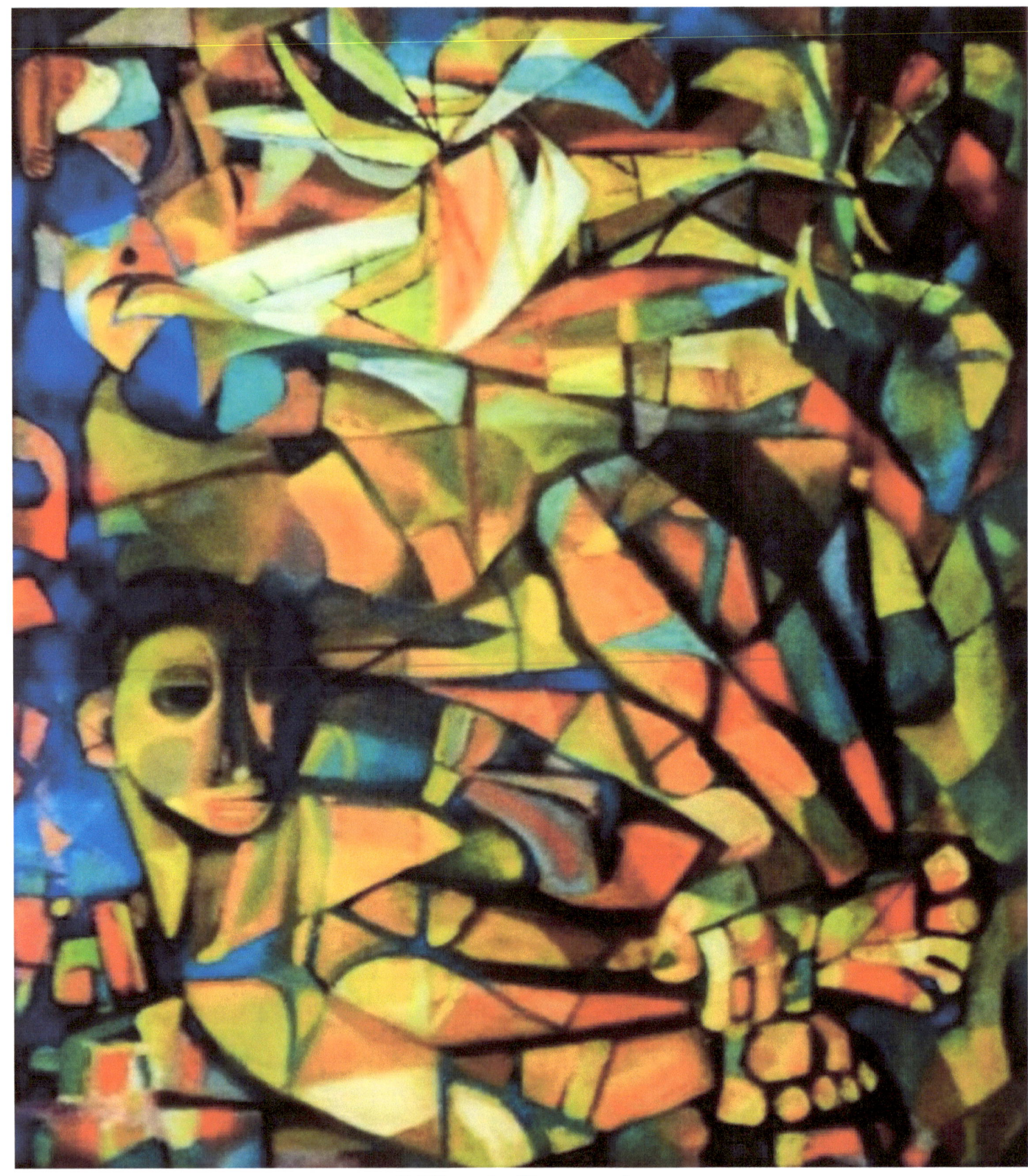

A Vicente Manansala

Fave Art - 17

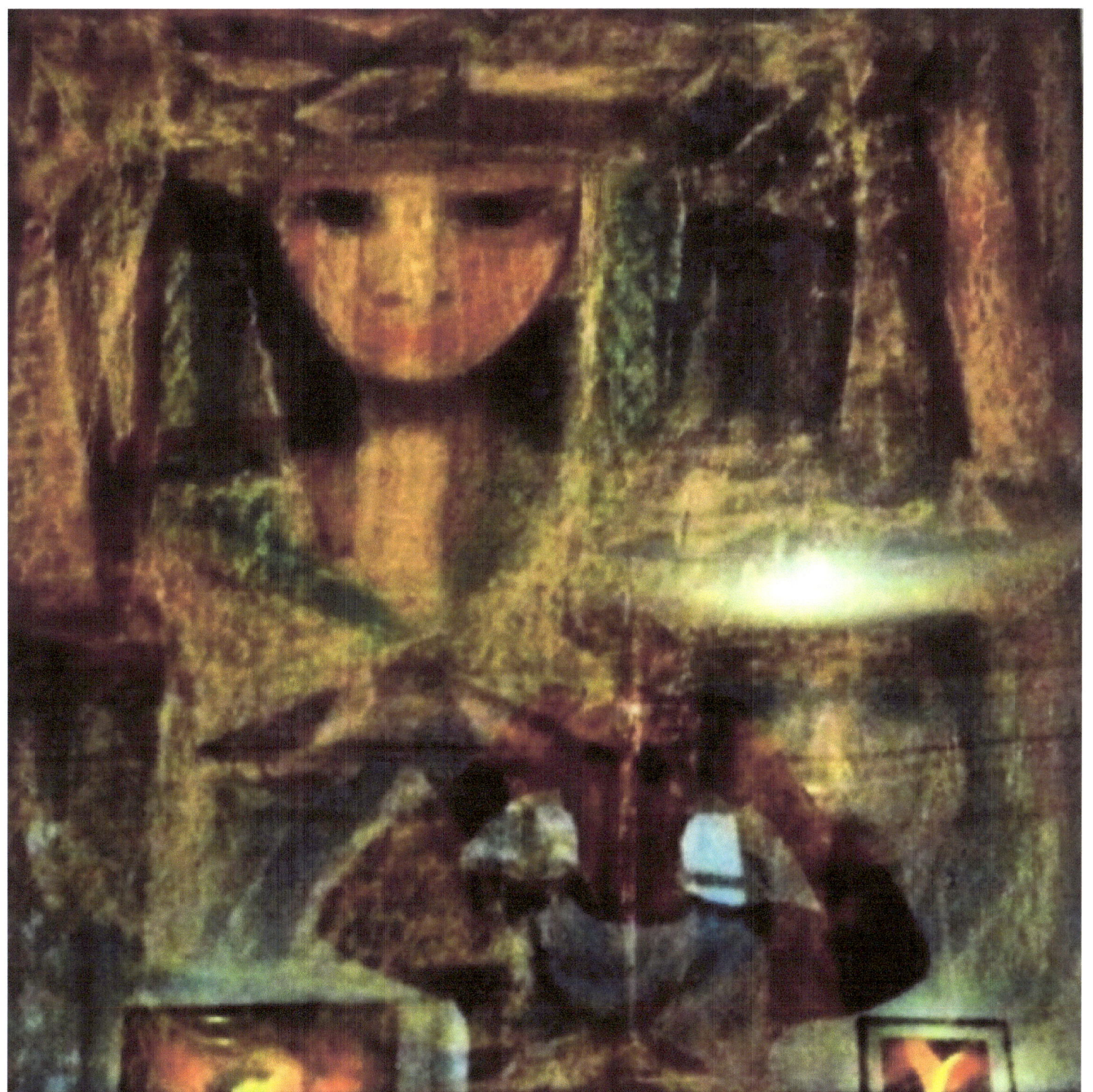

A Vicente Manansala

WELCOME! We hope you will enjoy this Fave Art-17 photo album of my favorite random collection of art. Photos are copied from the internet, posters, calendars, cards and art books. You may display this book as coffee table book in your living room, as conversation piece. You may give this as gift. You may cut out each page, 8.5x11 inches, for framing. Printed by Tatay Jobo Elizes under following ISBN Code Numbers:

Fave Art - 17

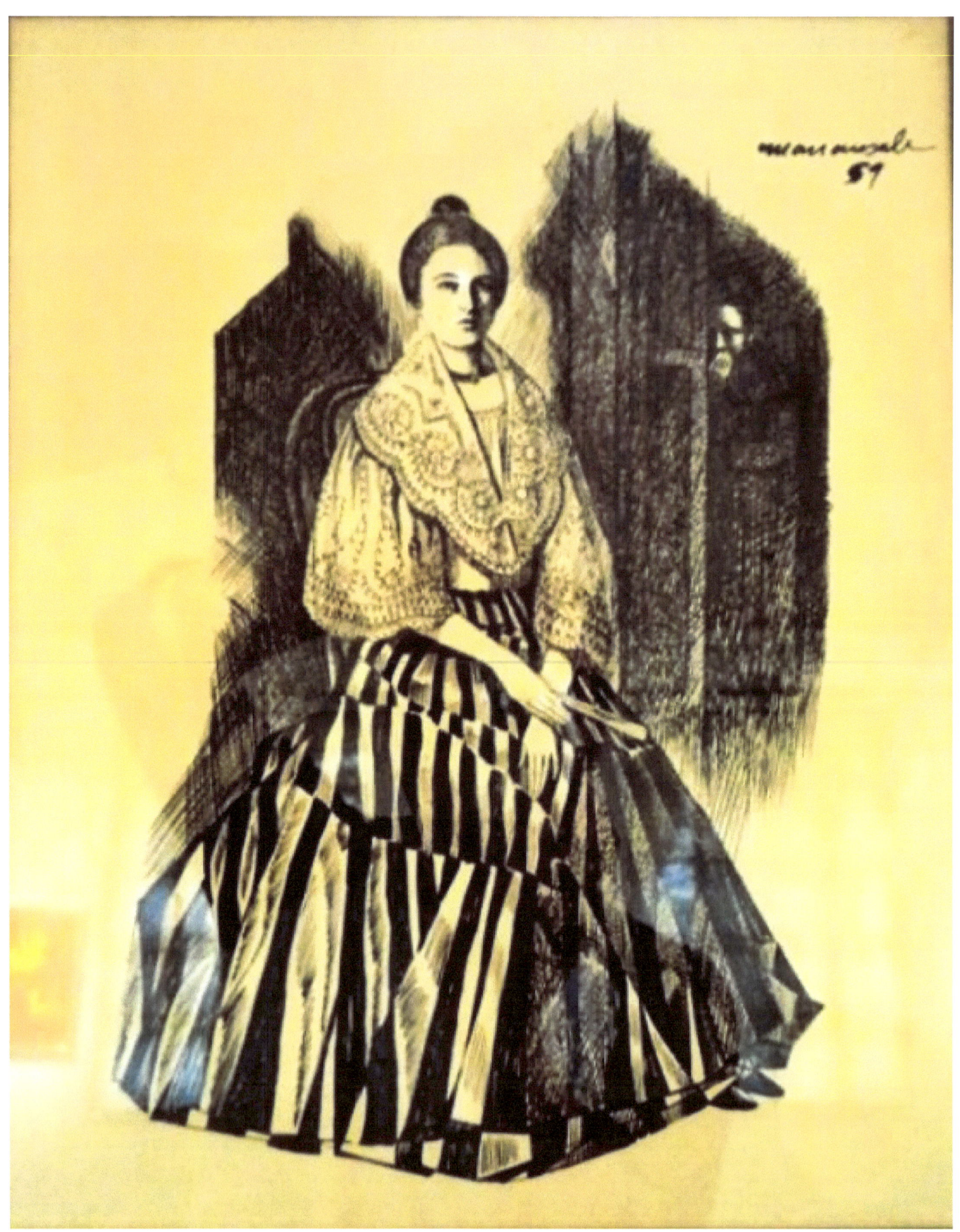

A Vicente Manansala, 1959

Fave Art - 17

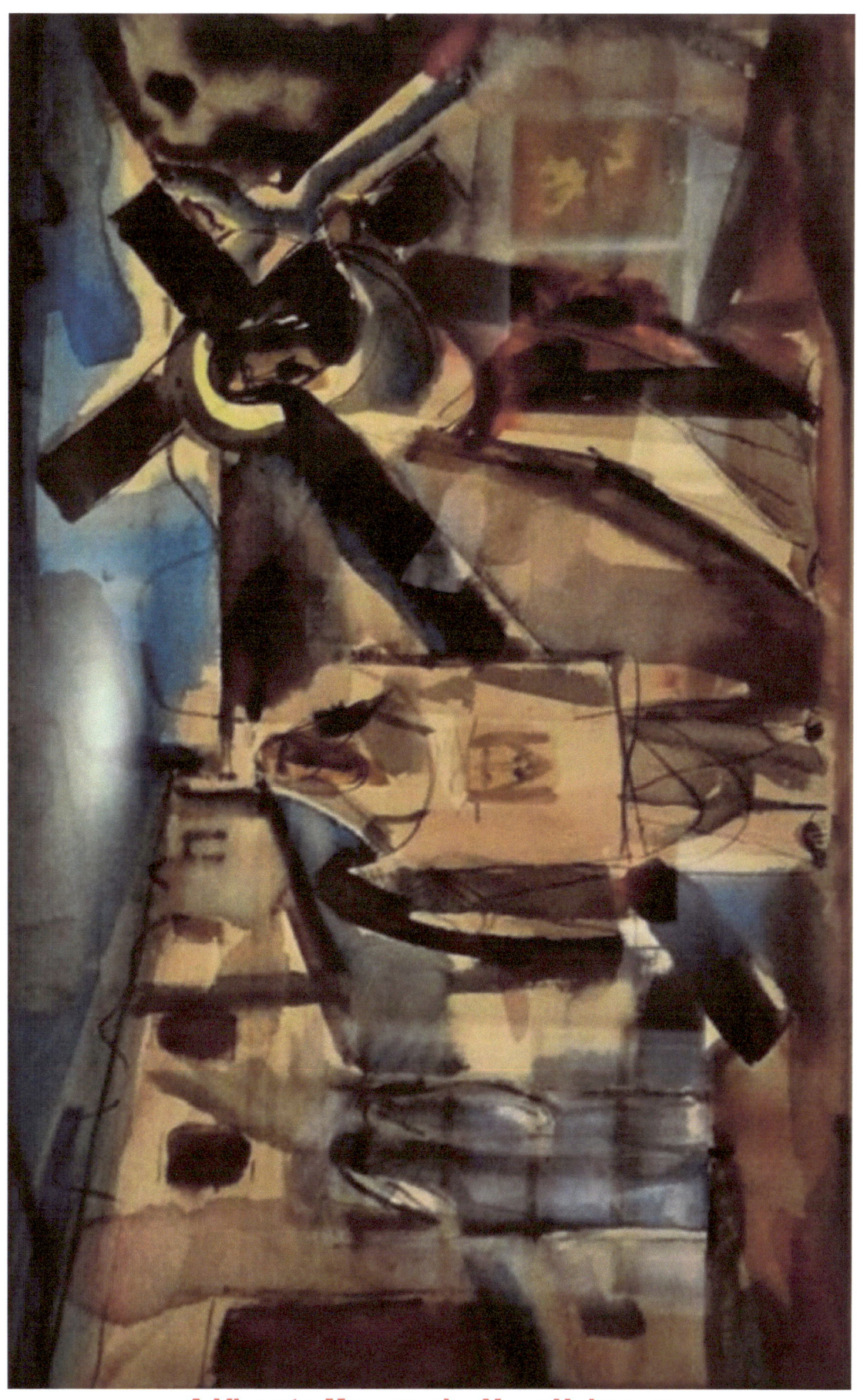

A Vicente Manansala, Year Unknown

Fave Art - 17

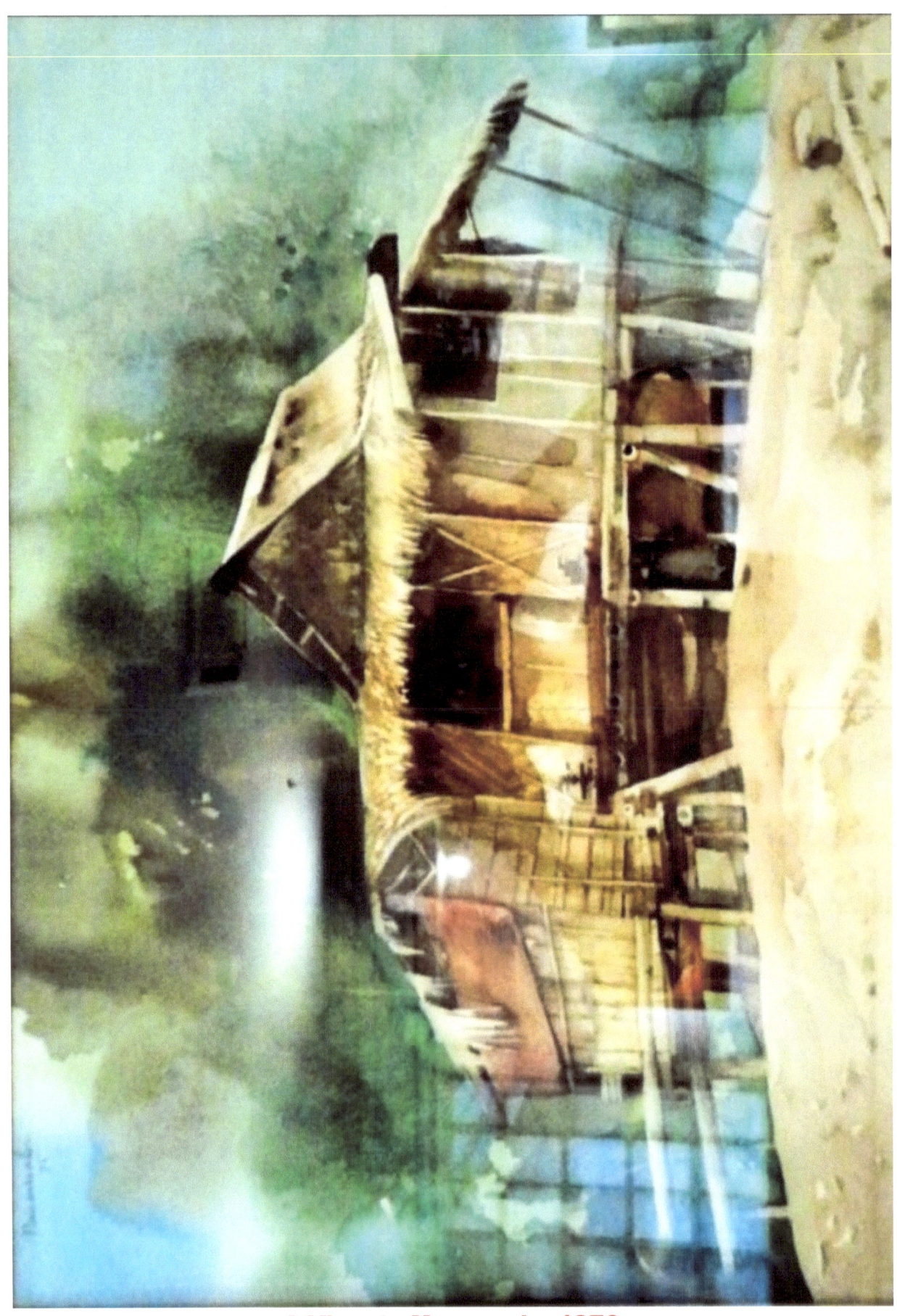

A Vicente Manansala, 1976

Fave Art - 17

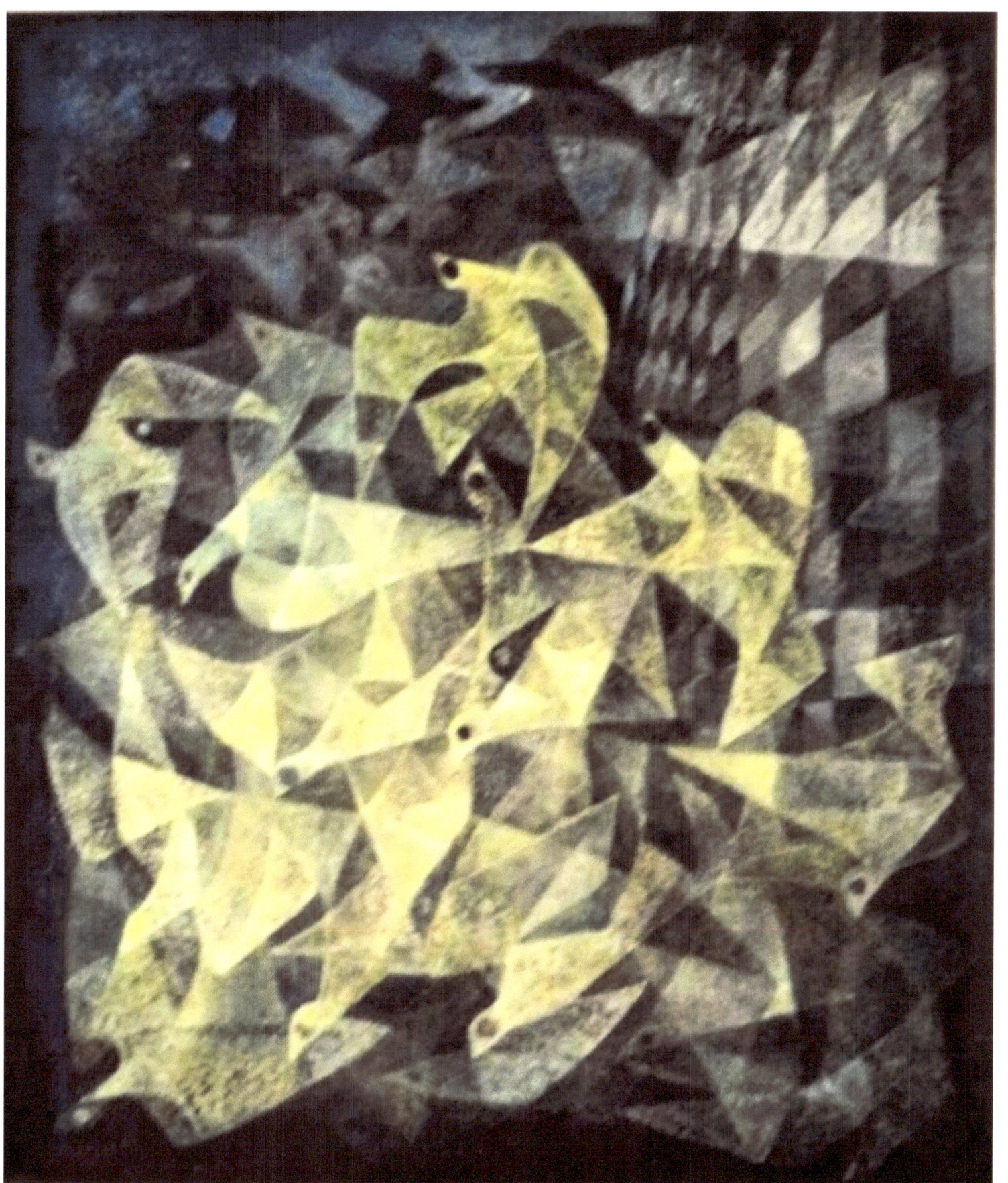

A Vicente Manansala, Year Unknown

Fave Art - 17

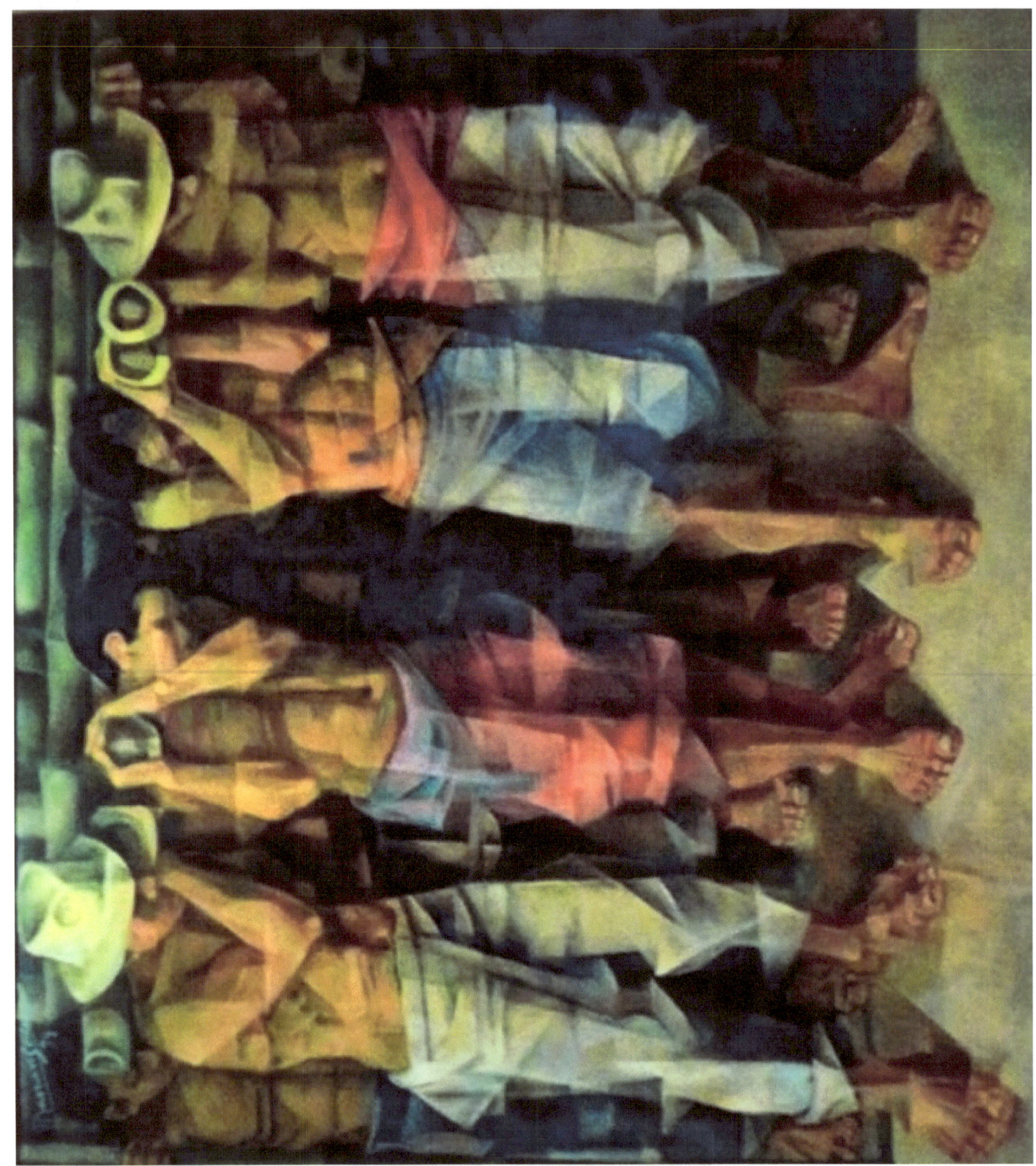

A Vicente Manansala, Year Unknown

Fave Art - 17

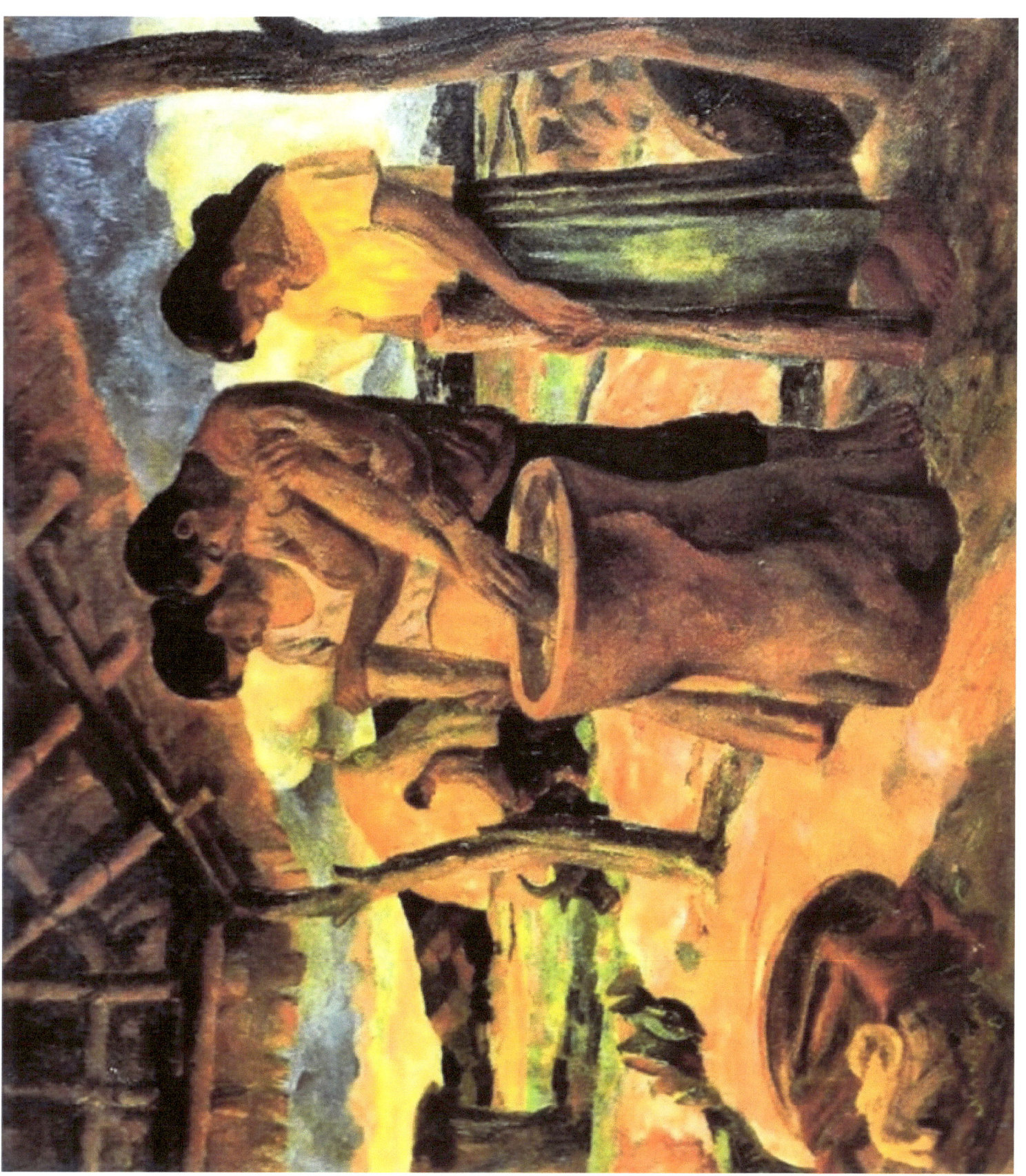

A Vicente Manansala, Year Unknown

Fave Art - 17

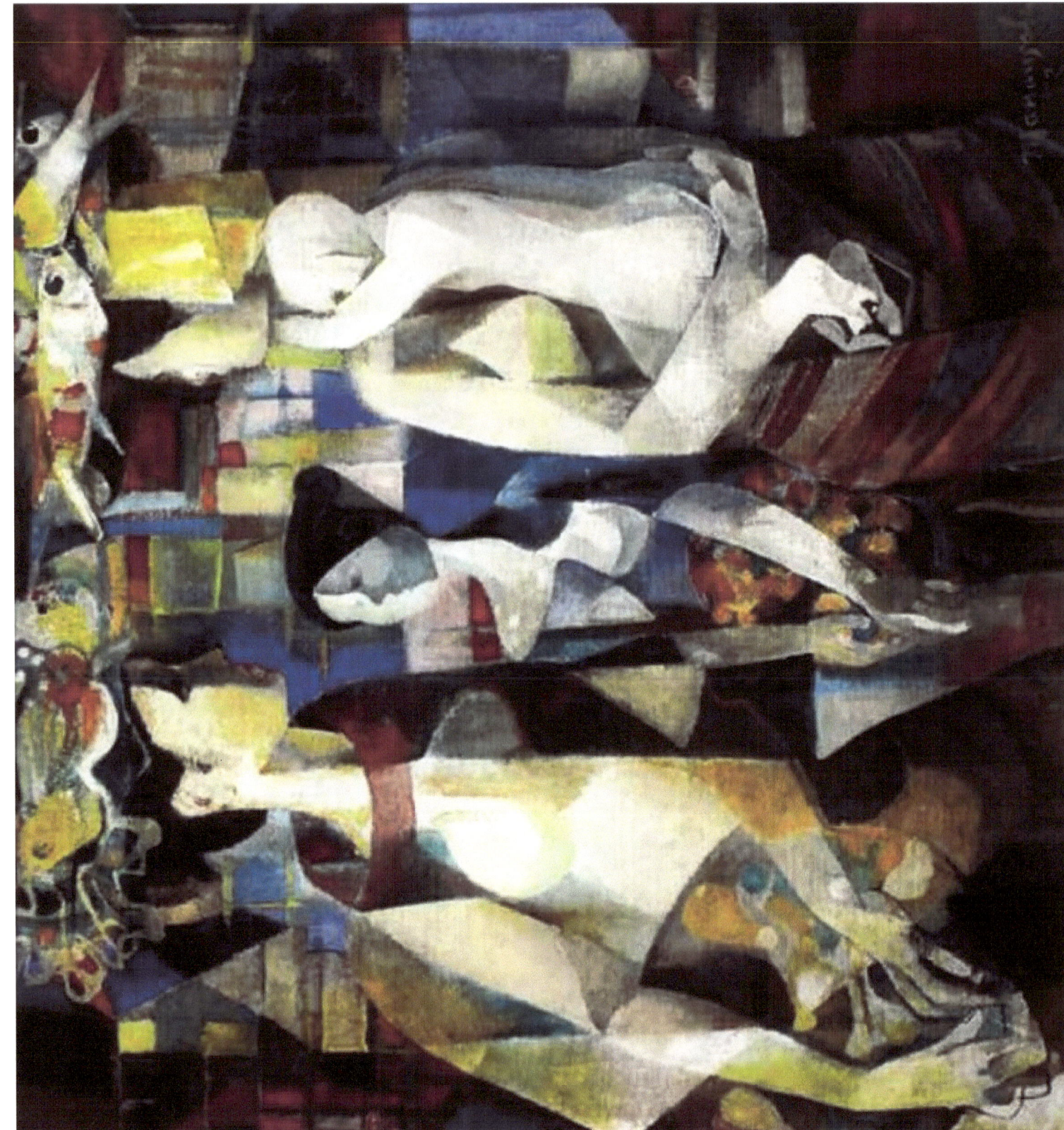

A Vicente Manansala, 1972

Fave Art - 17

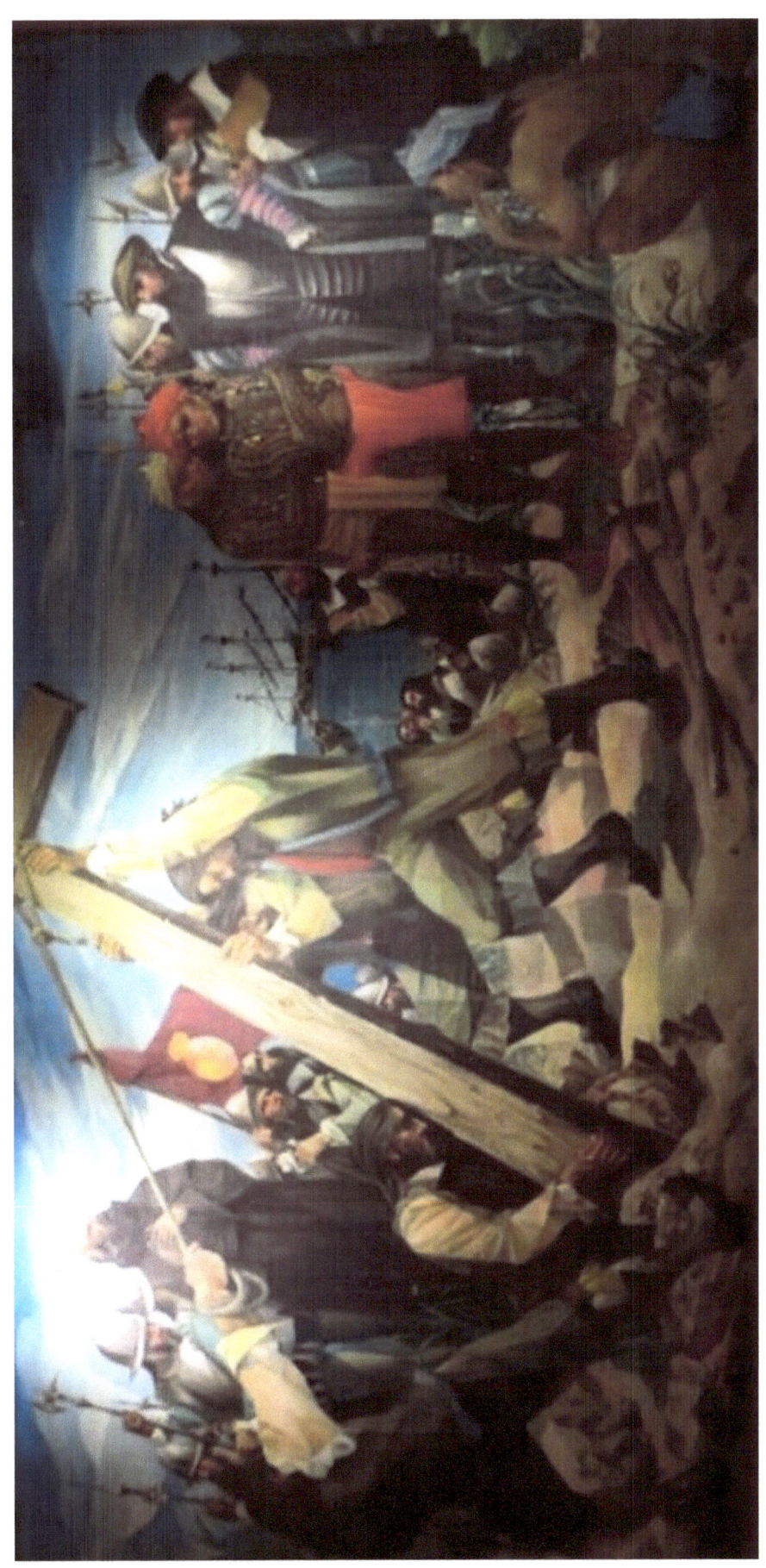

A Vicente Manansala or Botong Francisco?, Year Unknown

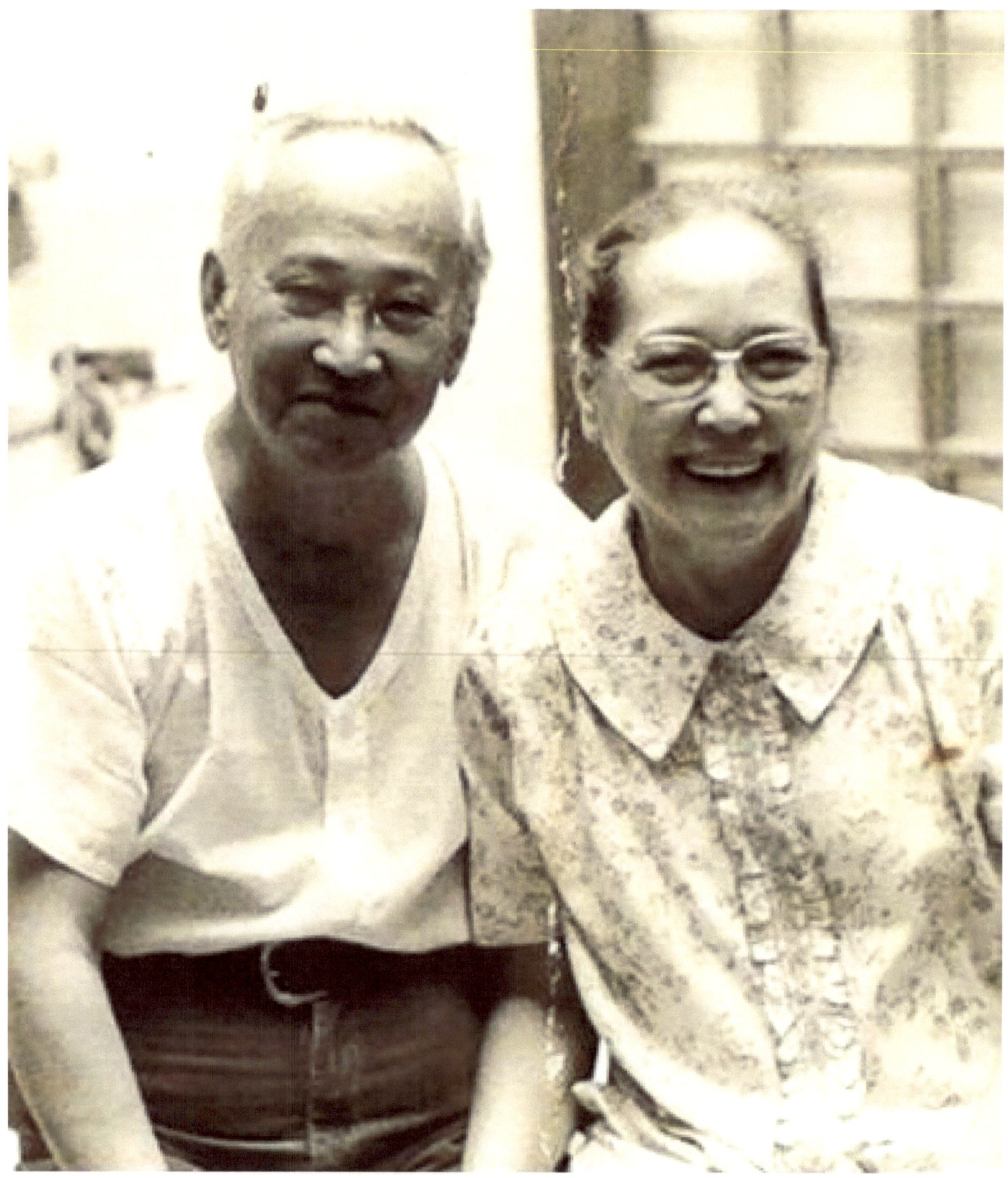

Mr. and Mrs. Vicente Manansala, for posterity

Fave Art - 17

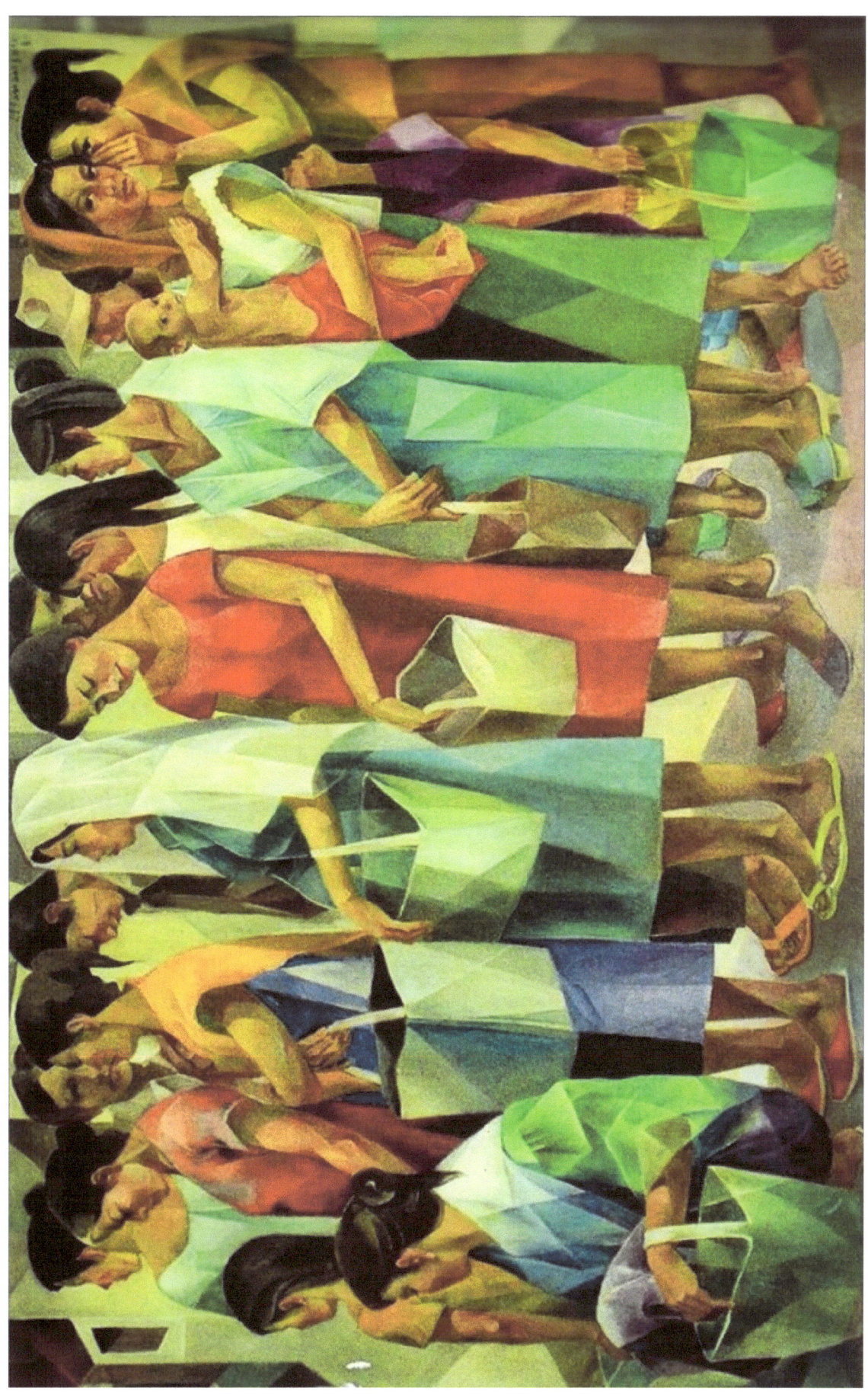

A Vicente Manansala, Year Unkno

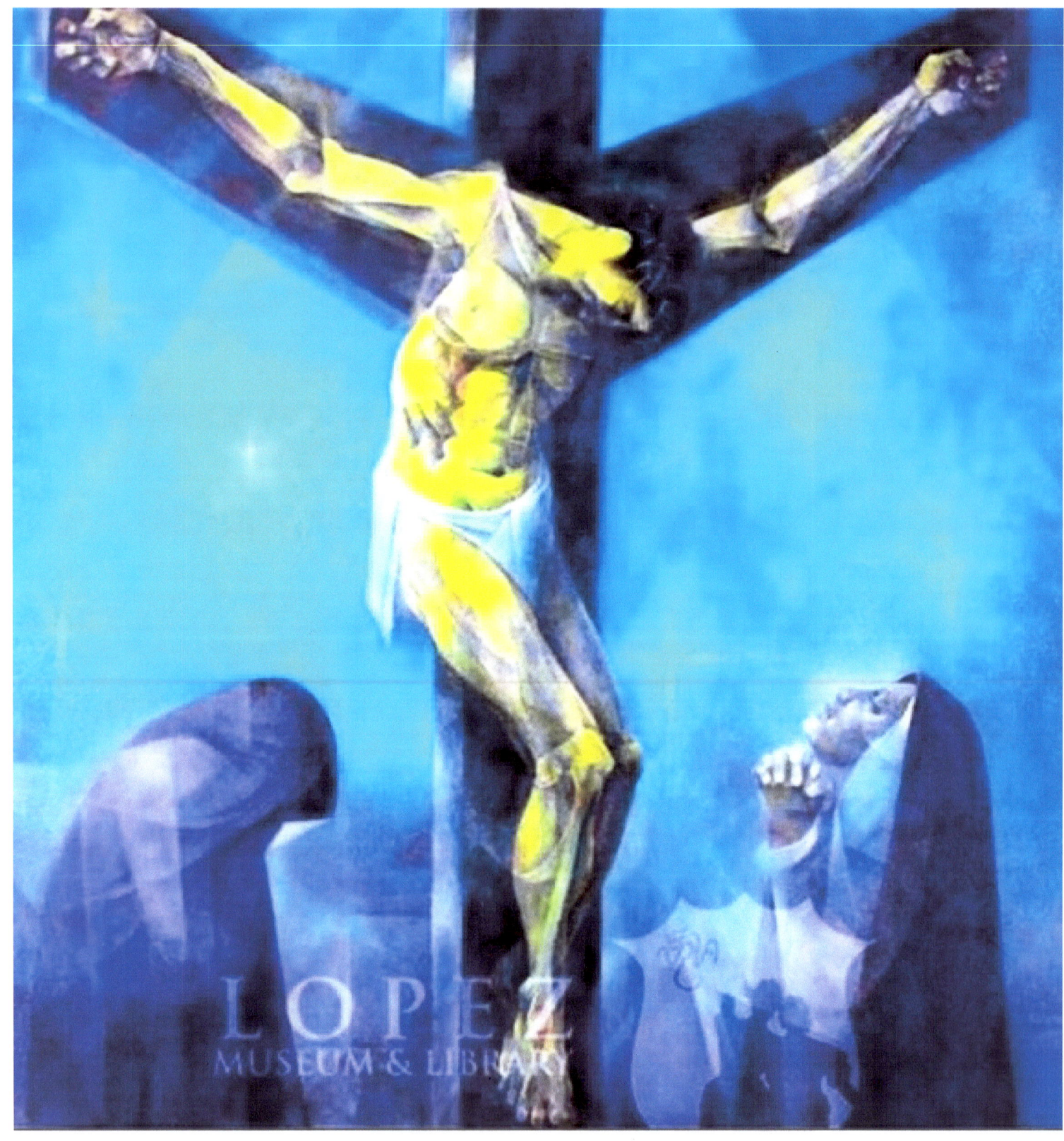

A Vicente Manansala, Year Unknown

Fave Art - 17

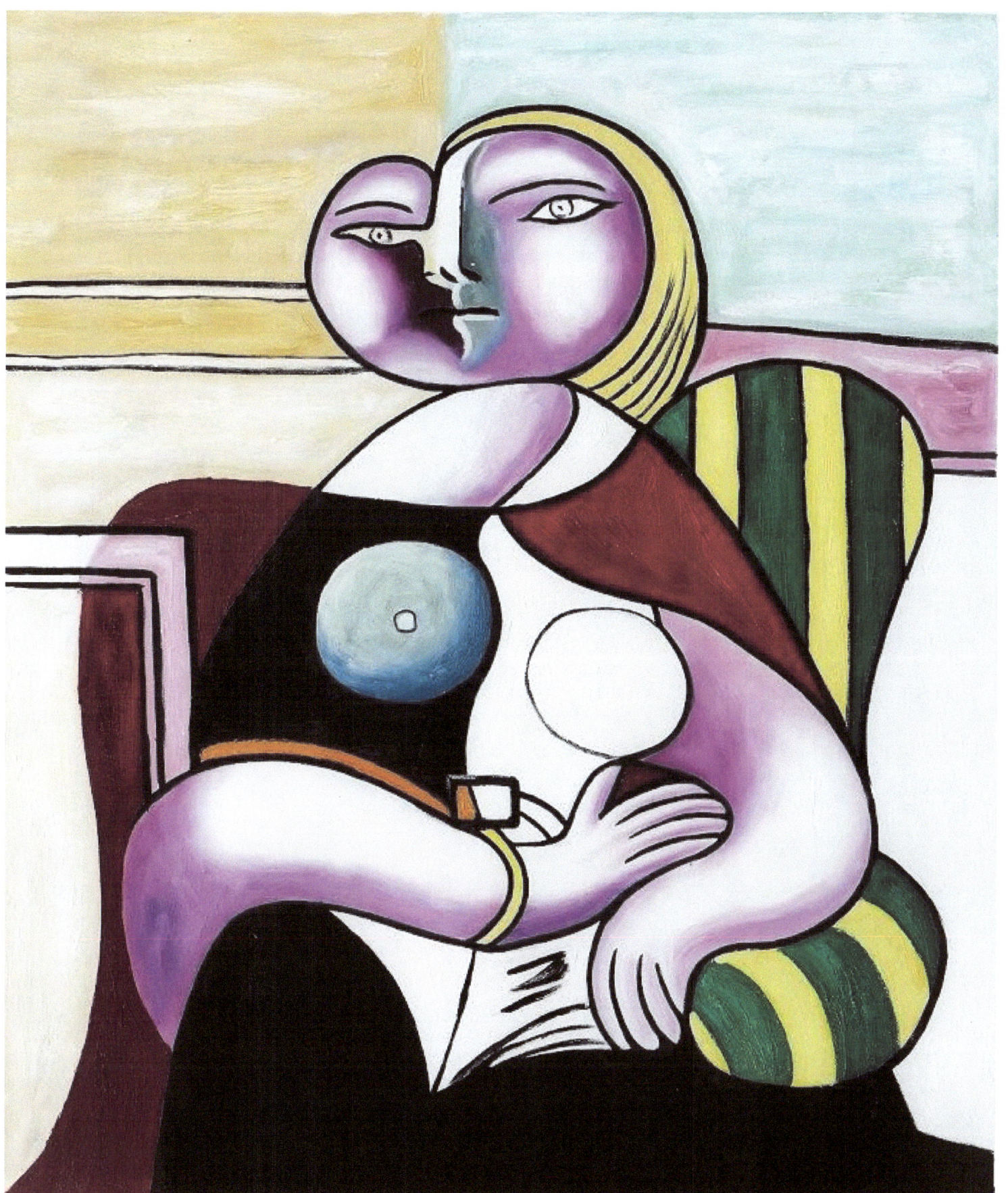

A Pablo Picasso, familiar style

Fave Art - 17

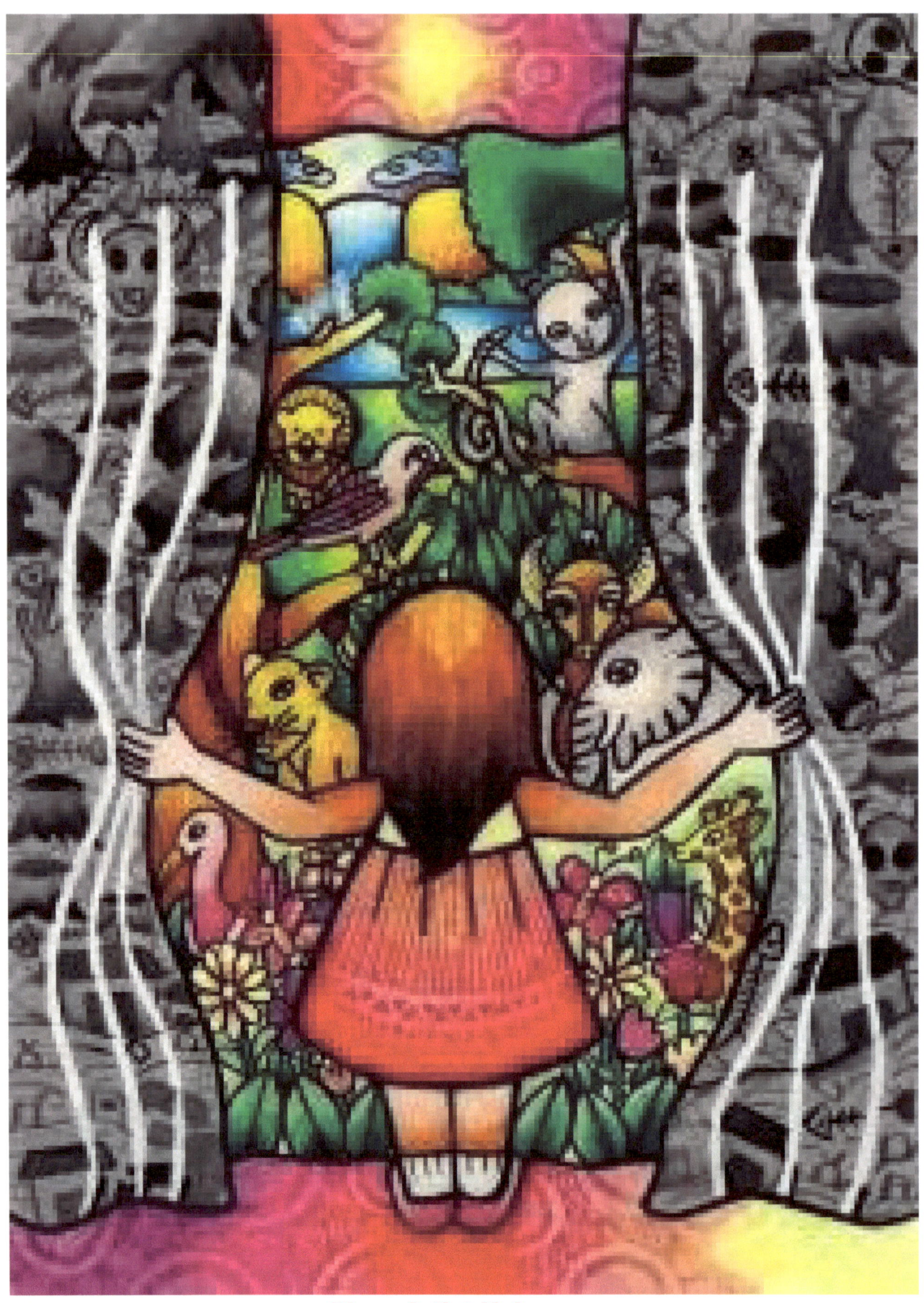

Pinoy Artist Unknown

Fave Art - 17

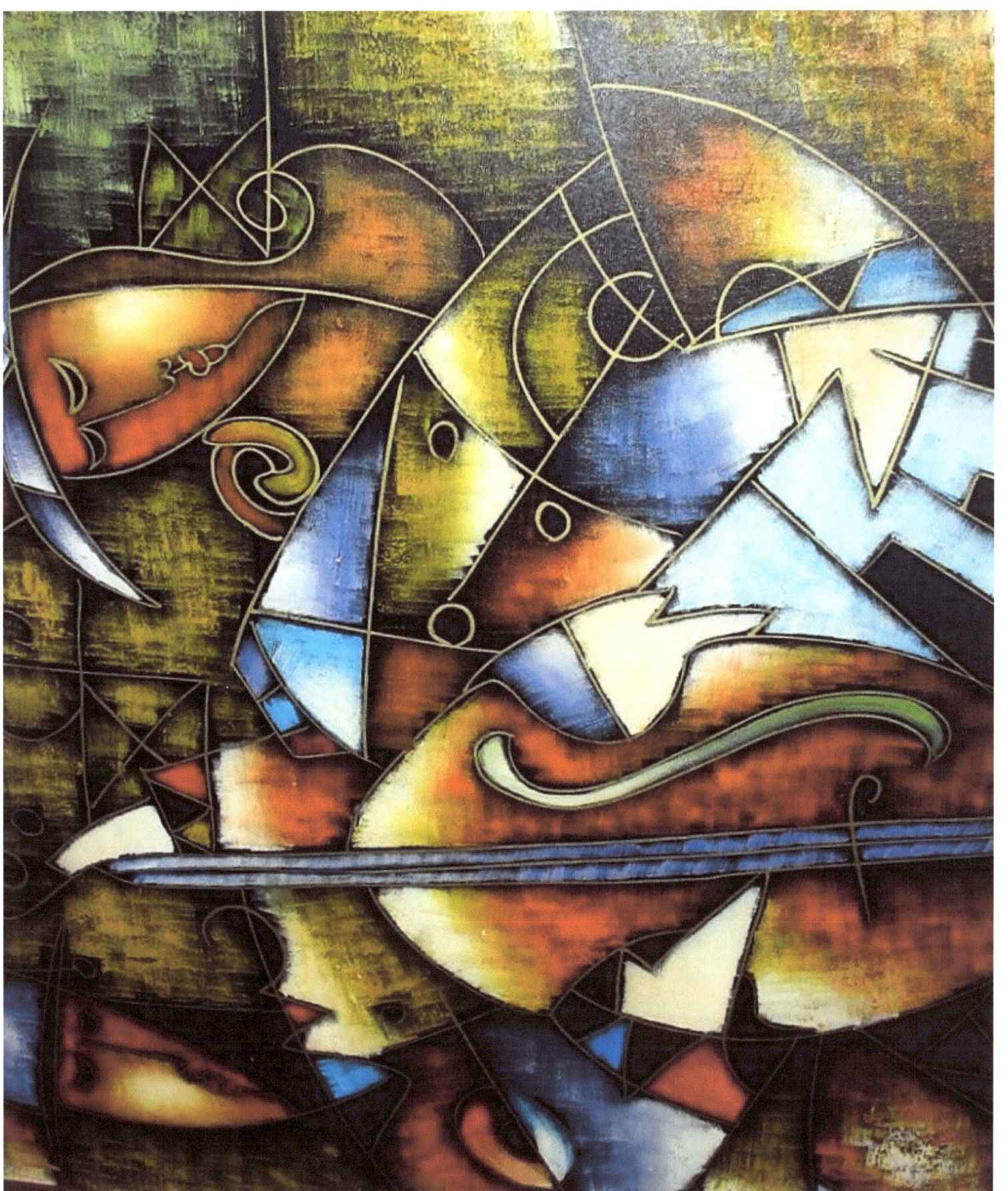

Pinoy Artist Unknown, modern painting

Fave Art - 17

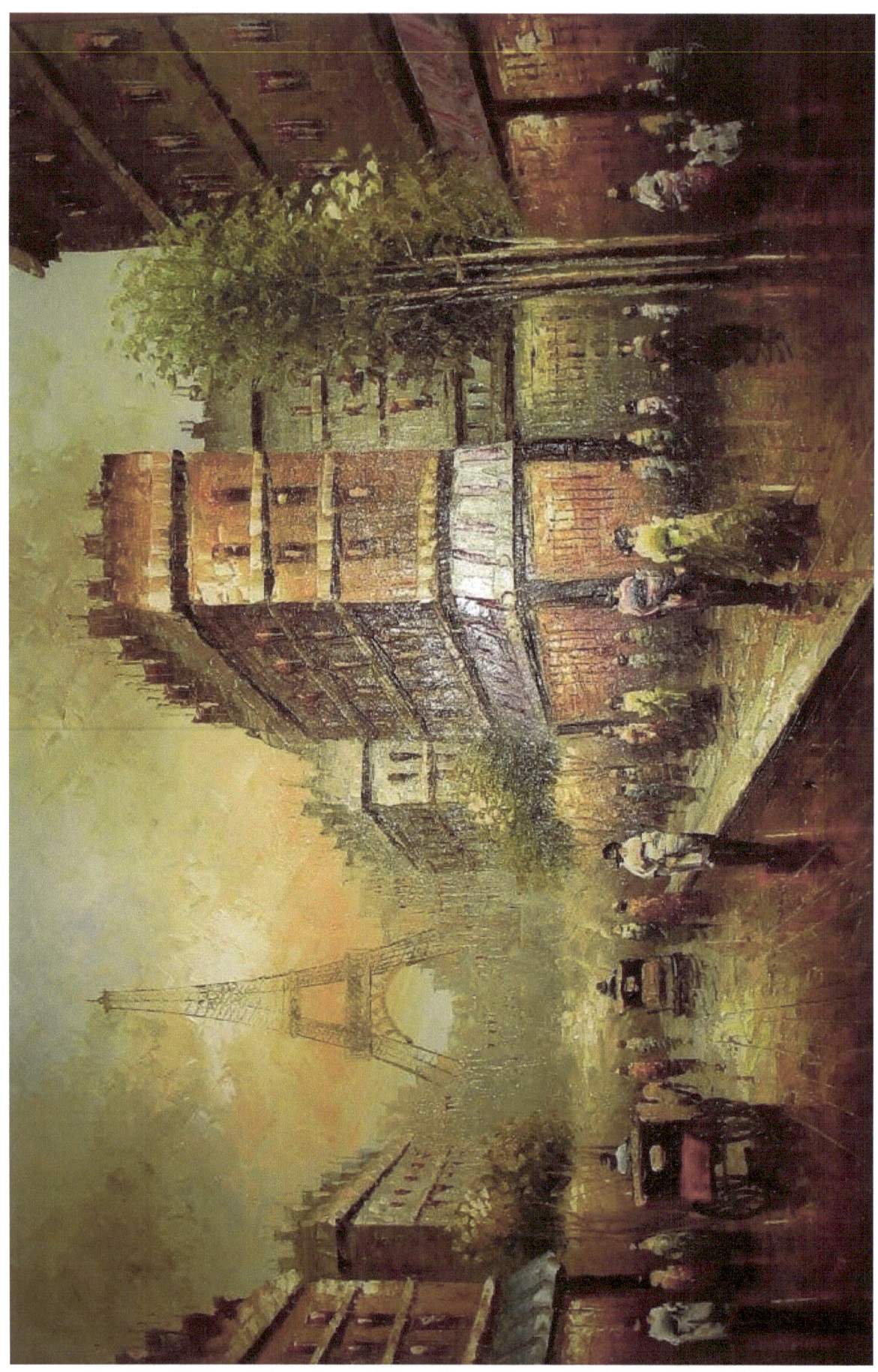

Looks like a Renoir or Monet or Manet? (classic paintin

Fave Art - 17

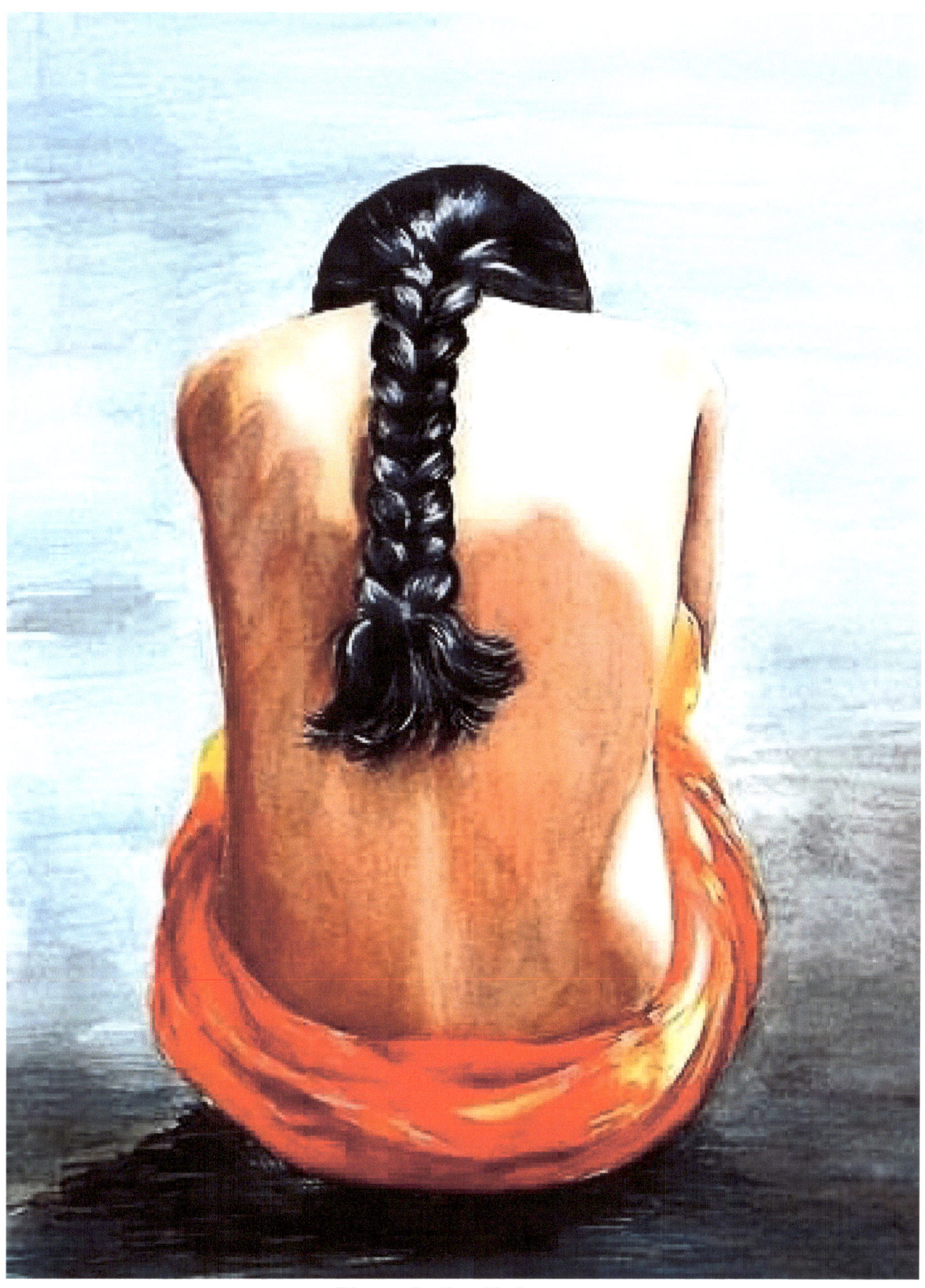

Pinoy Artist Unknown

Fave Art - 17

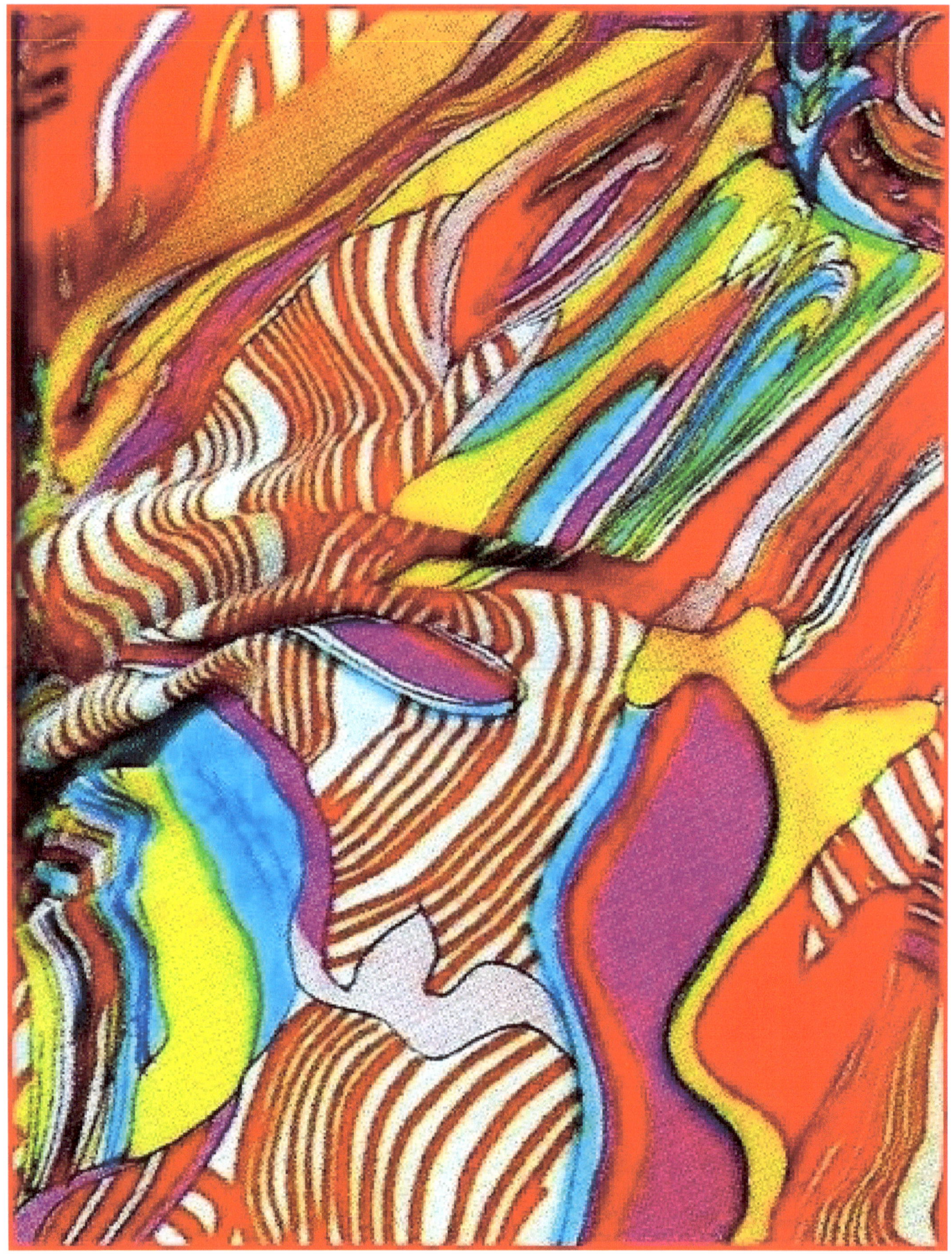

Pinoy Artist U

Fave Art - 17

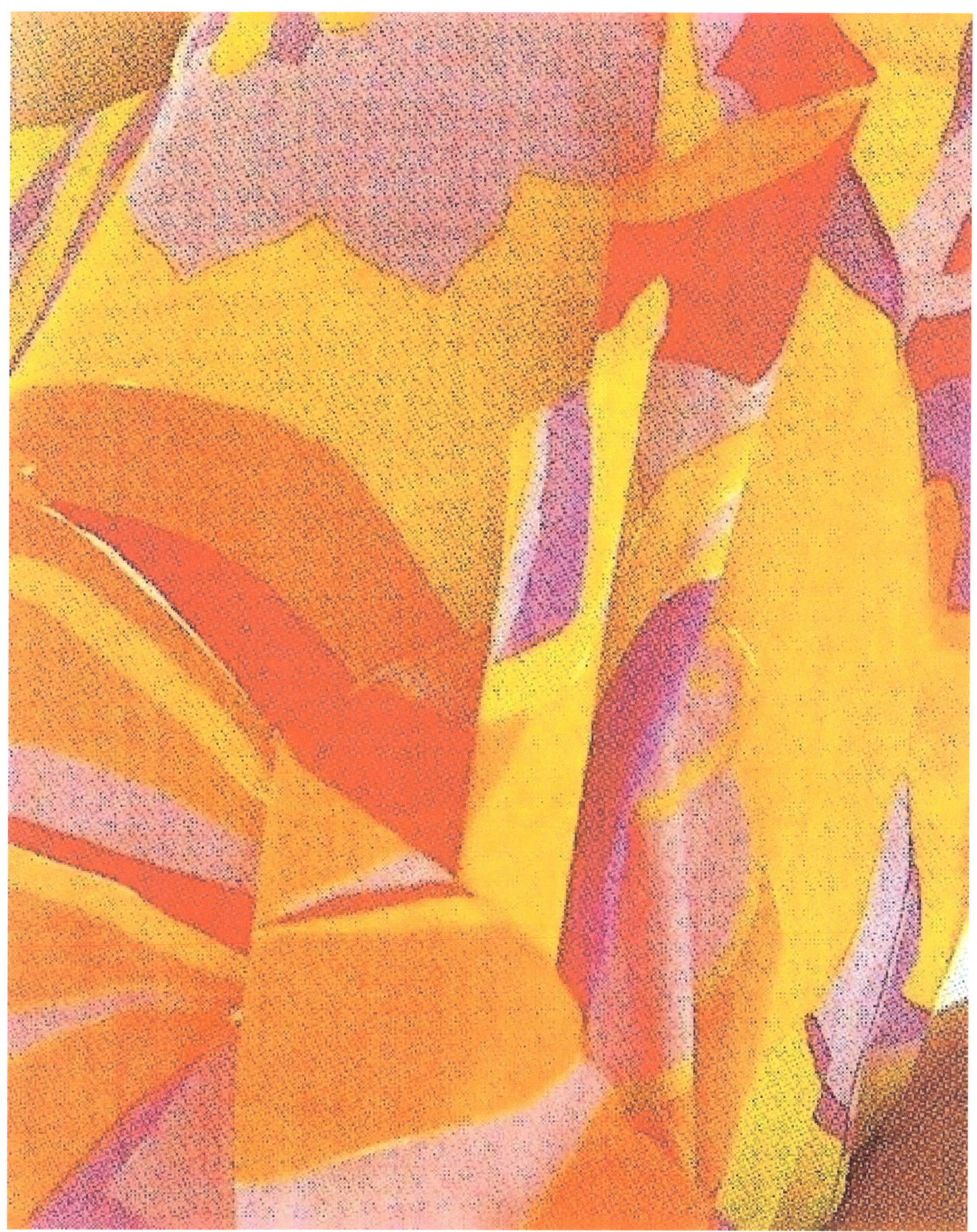

Pinoy Artist Unknown

Fave Art - 17

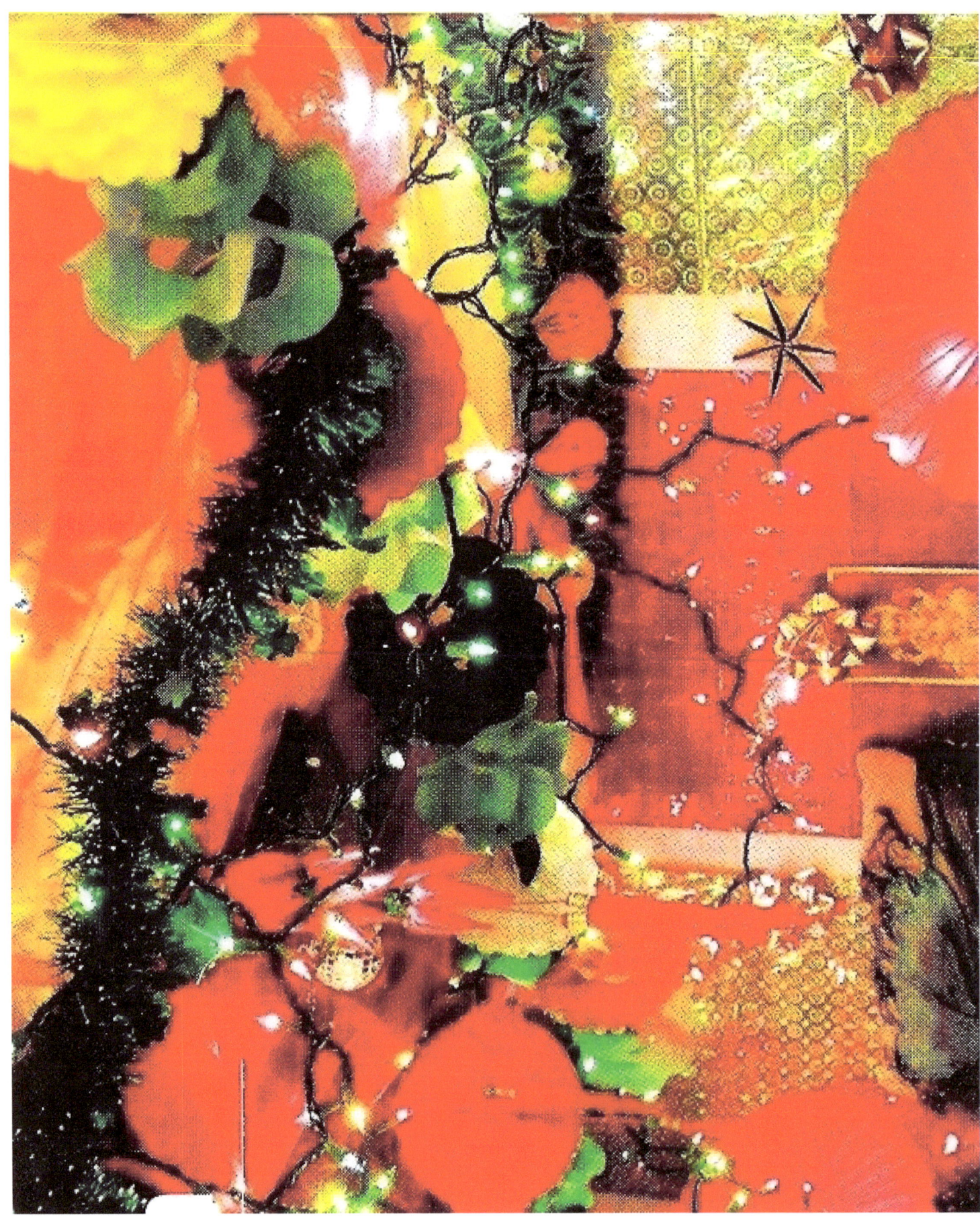

Pinoy Artist Unknown

Fave Art - 17

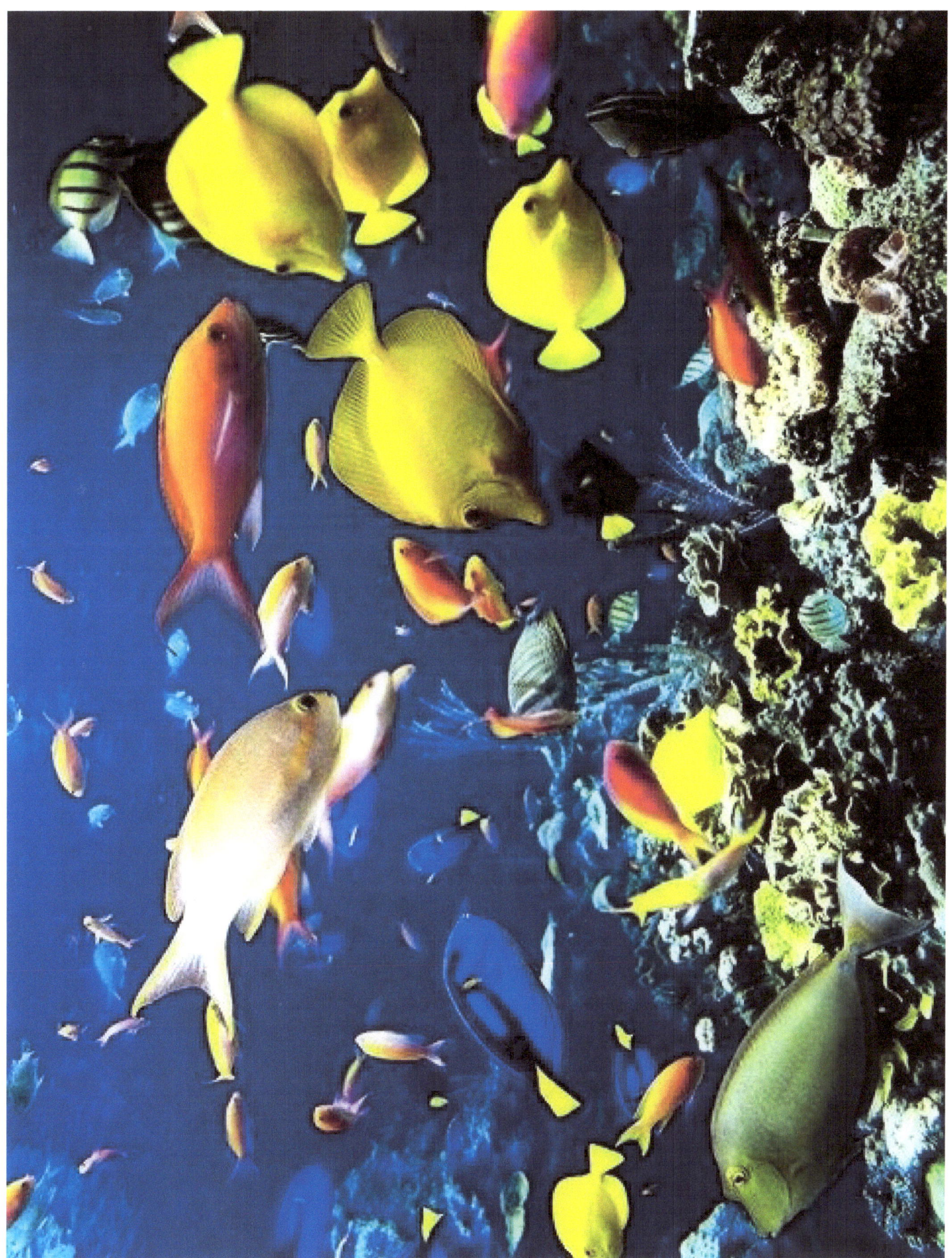

Pinoy Artist Unknow

Fave Art - 17

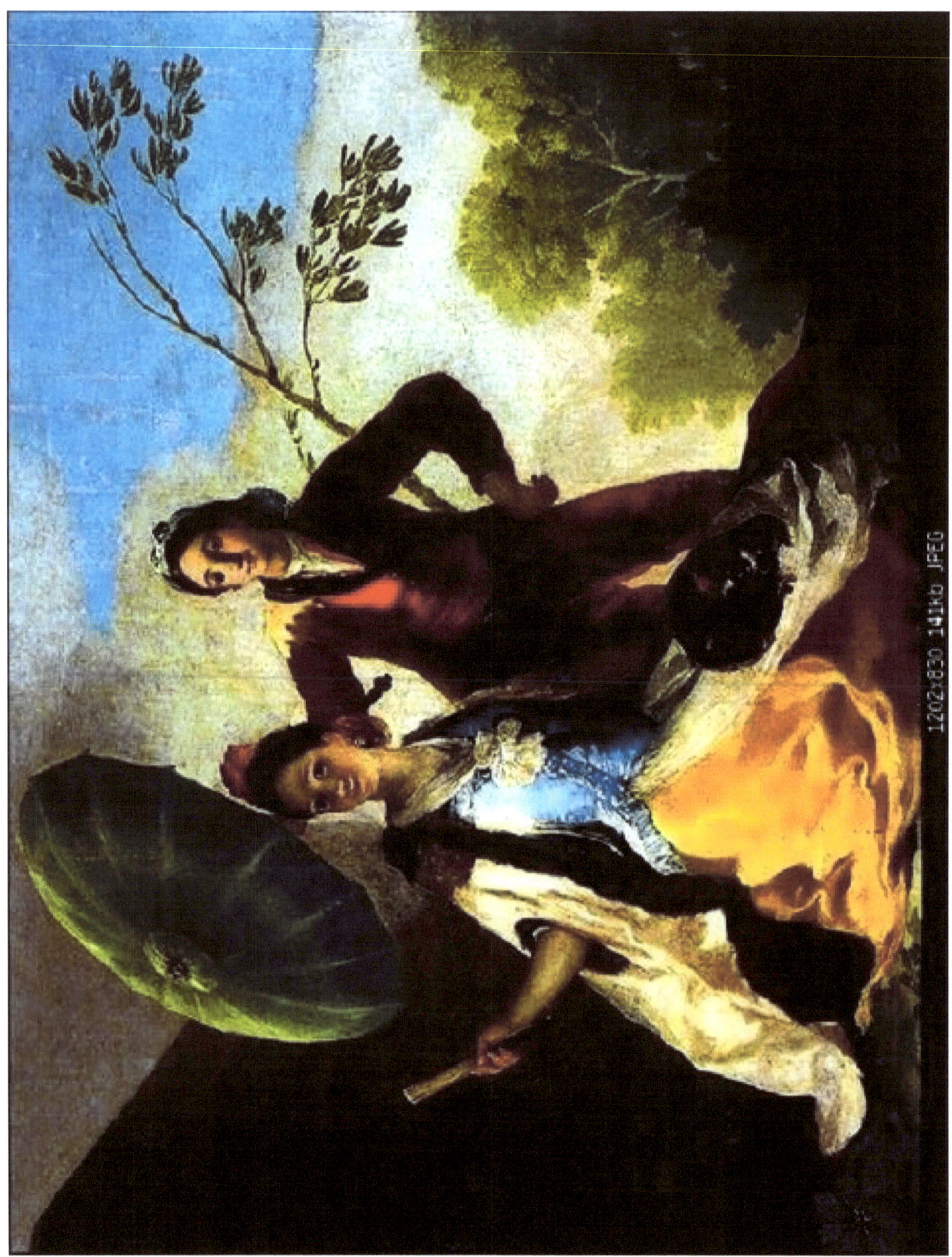

Artist Unknown

Fave Art - 17

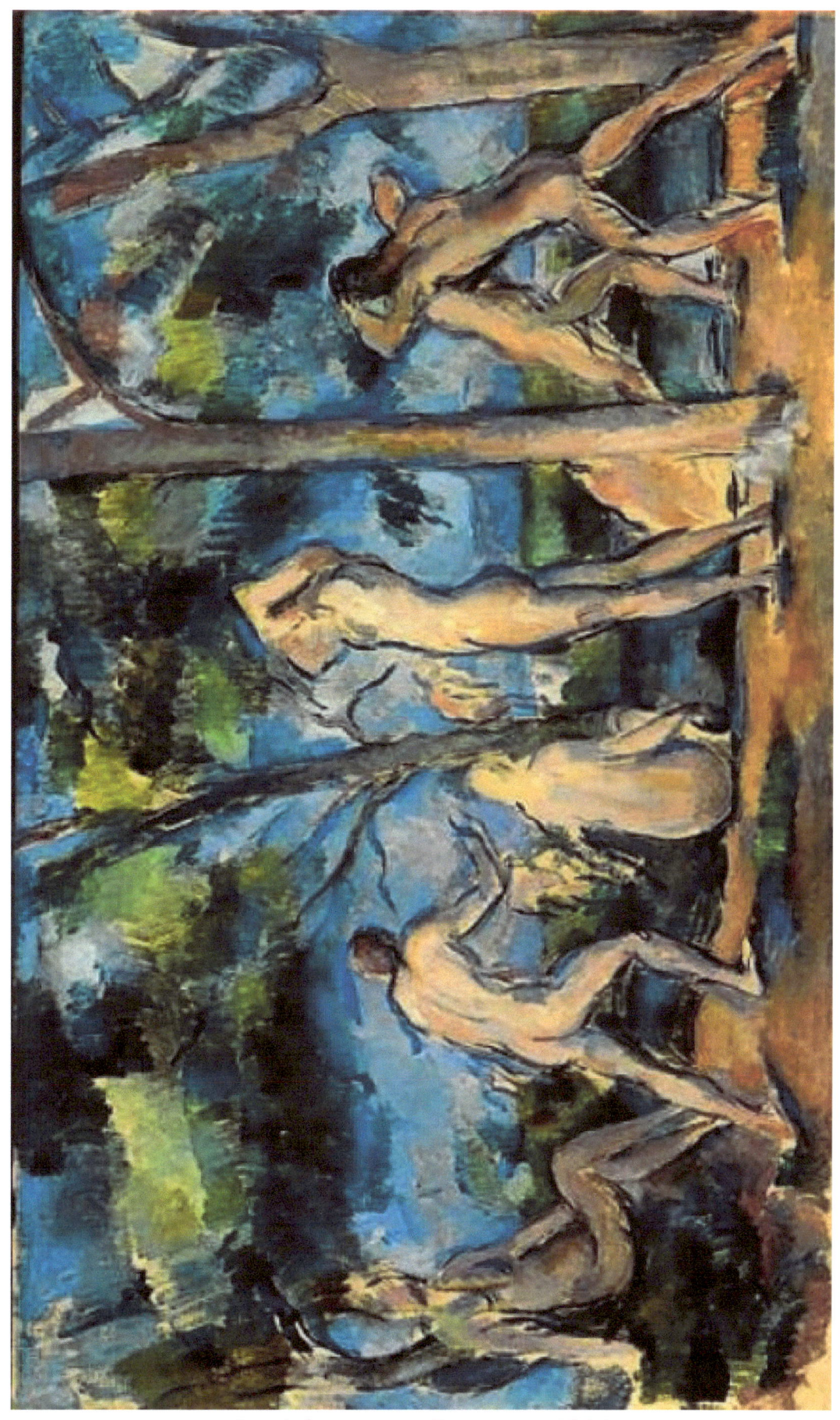

Paul Cezanne, Bathers, 1898

Fave Art - 17

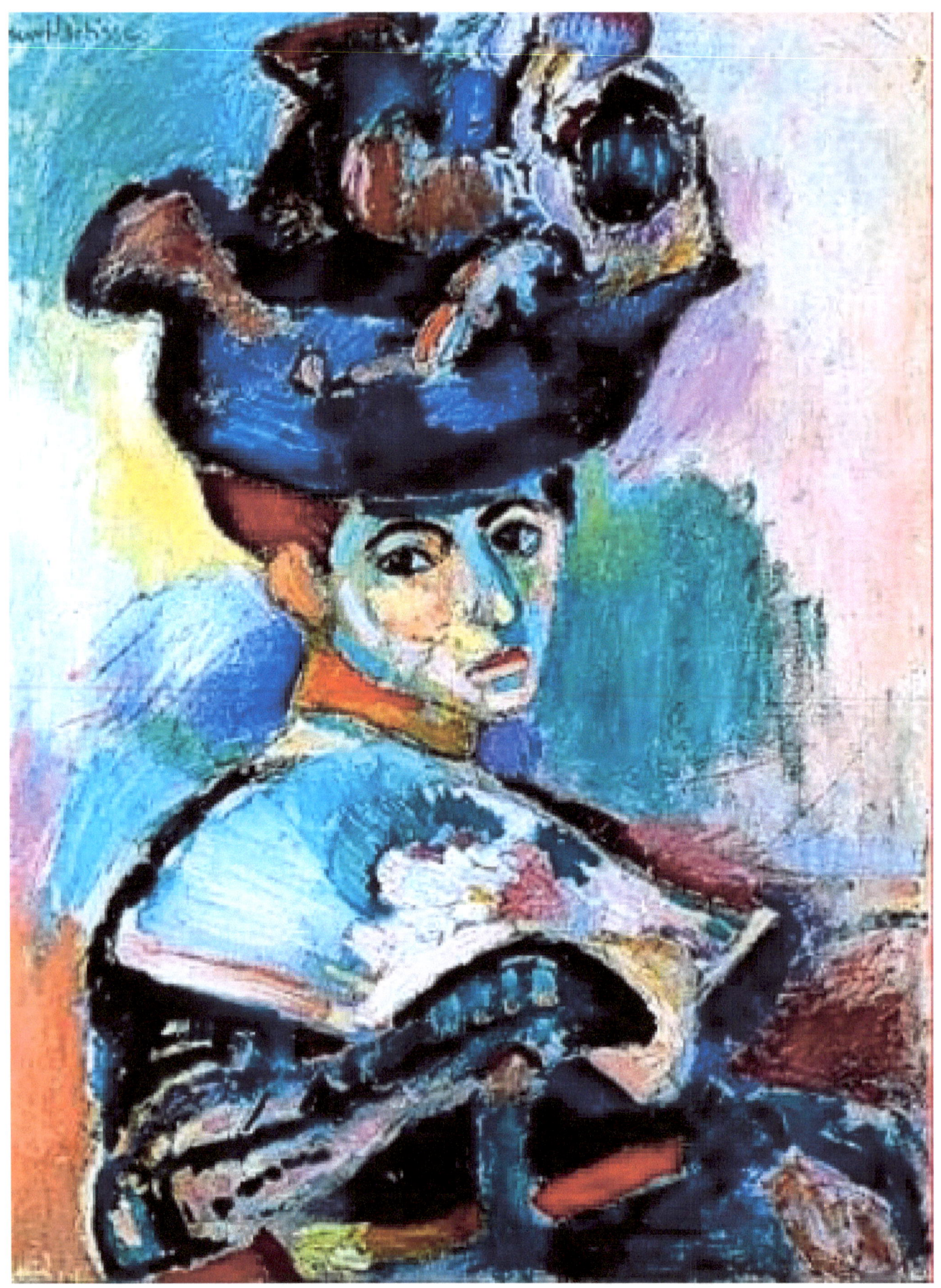

Henri Matisse, Woman with a Heart, 189

Fave Art - 17

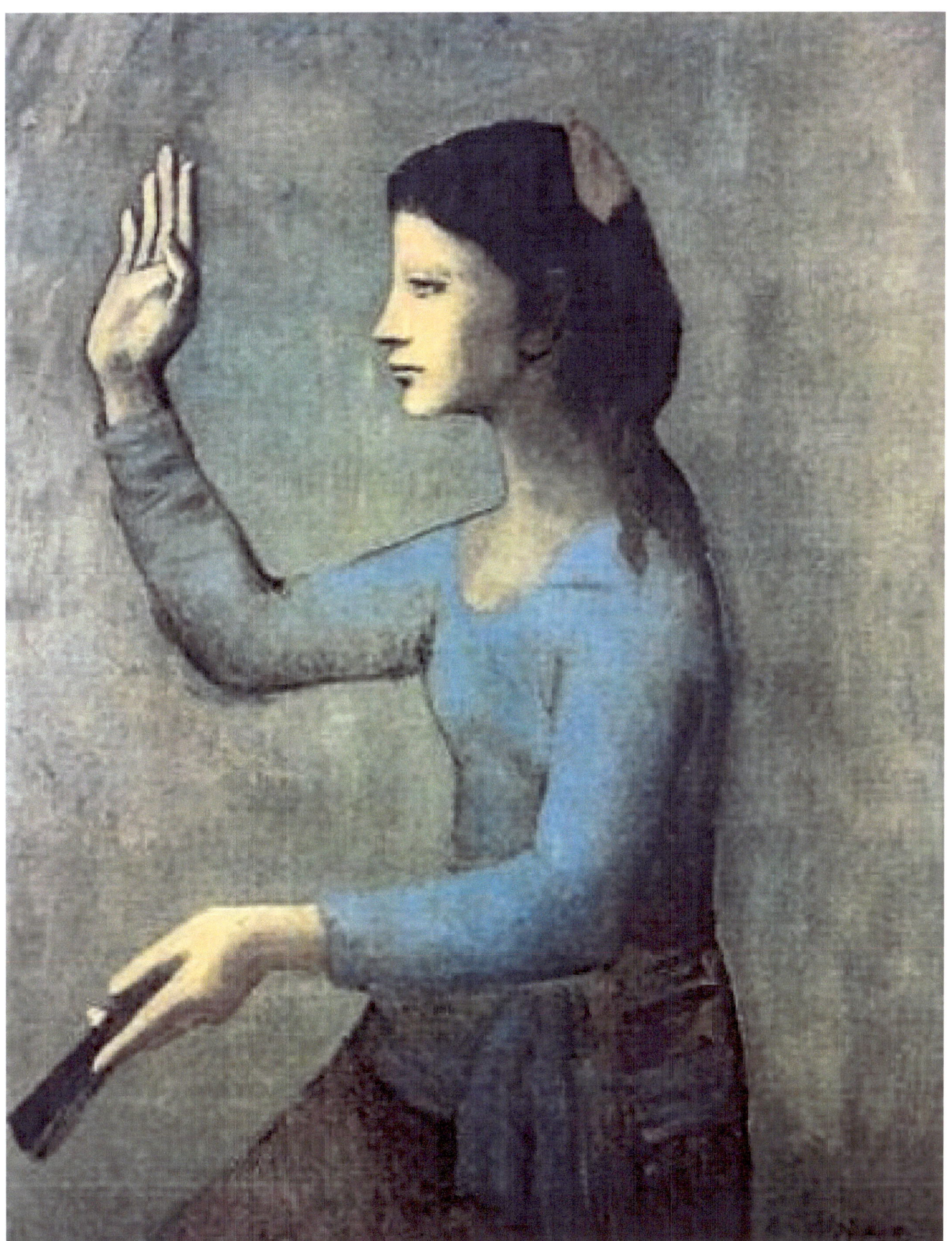

Pablo Picasso, Lady with a Fan, 1905

Fave Art - 17

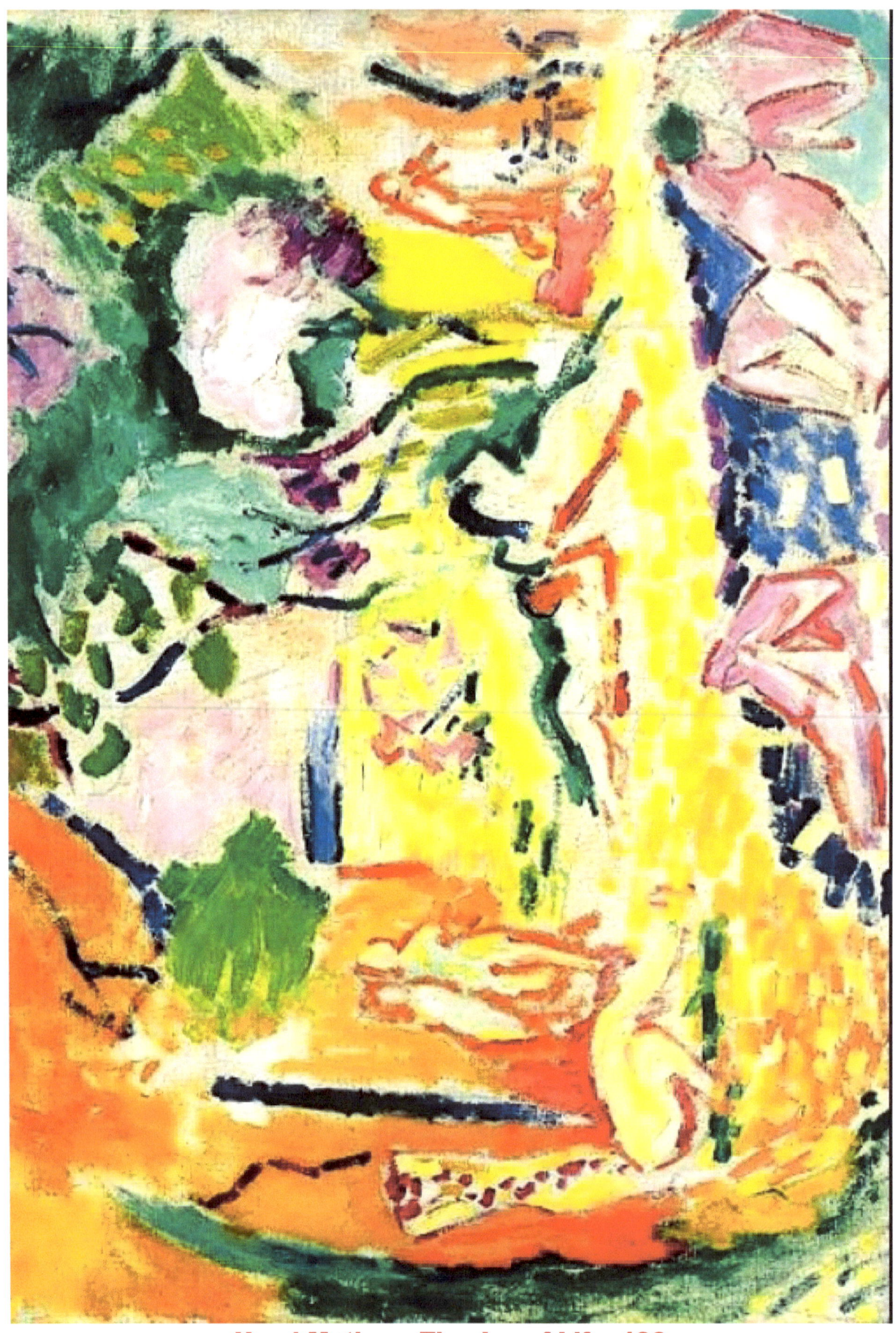

Henri Matisse, The Joy of Life, 190

Fave Art - 17

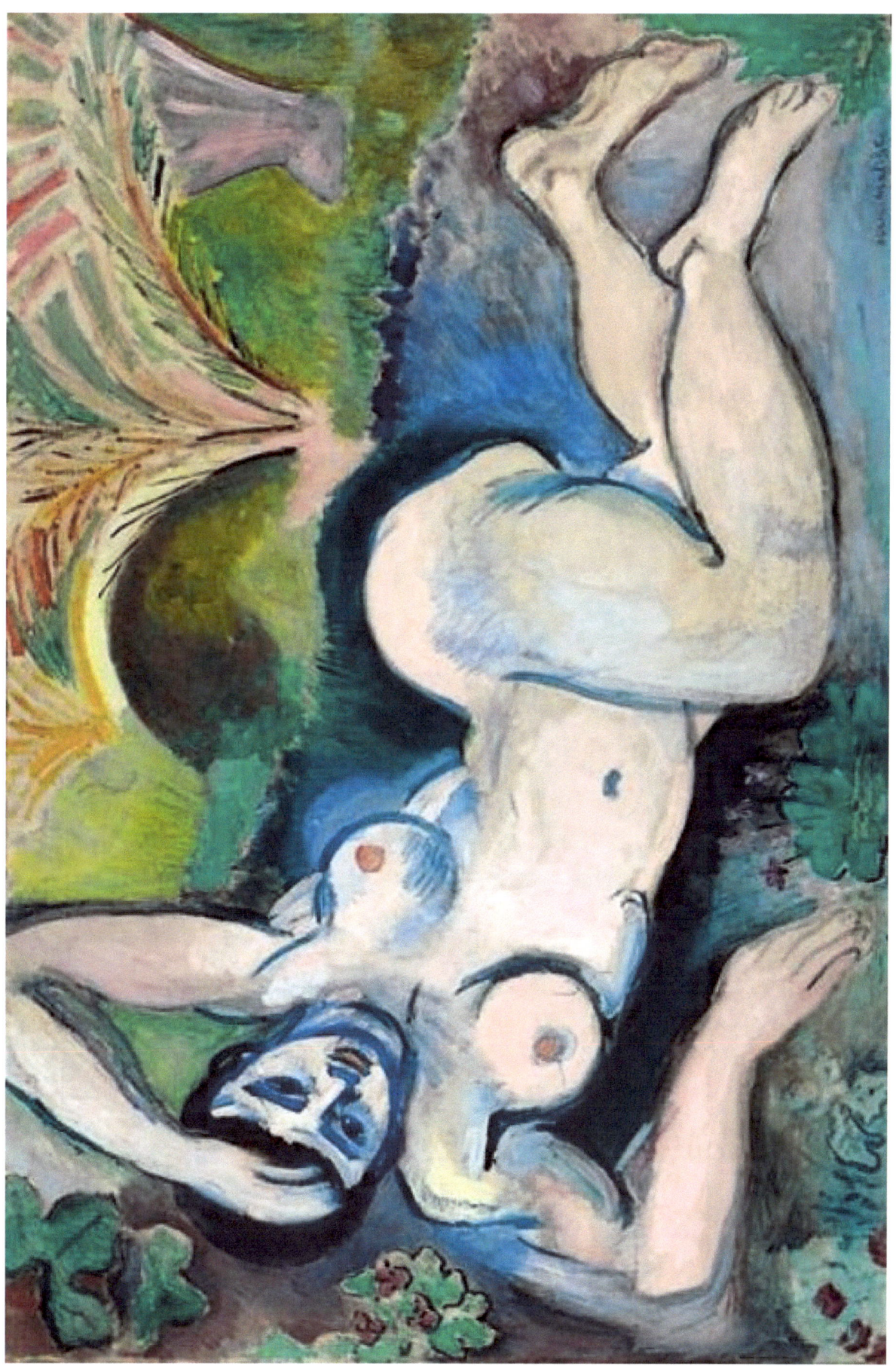

Henri Matisse, Blue Nude, 1905

Fave Art - 17

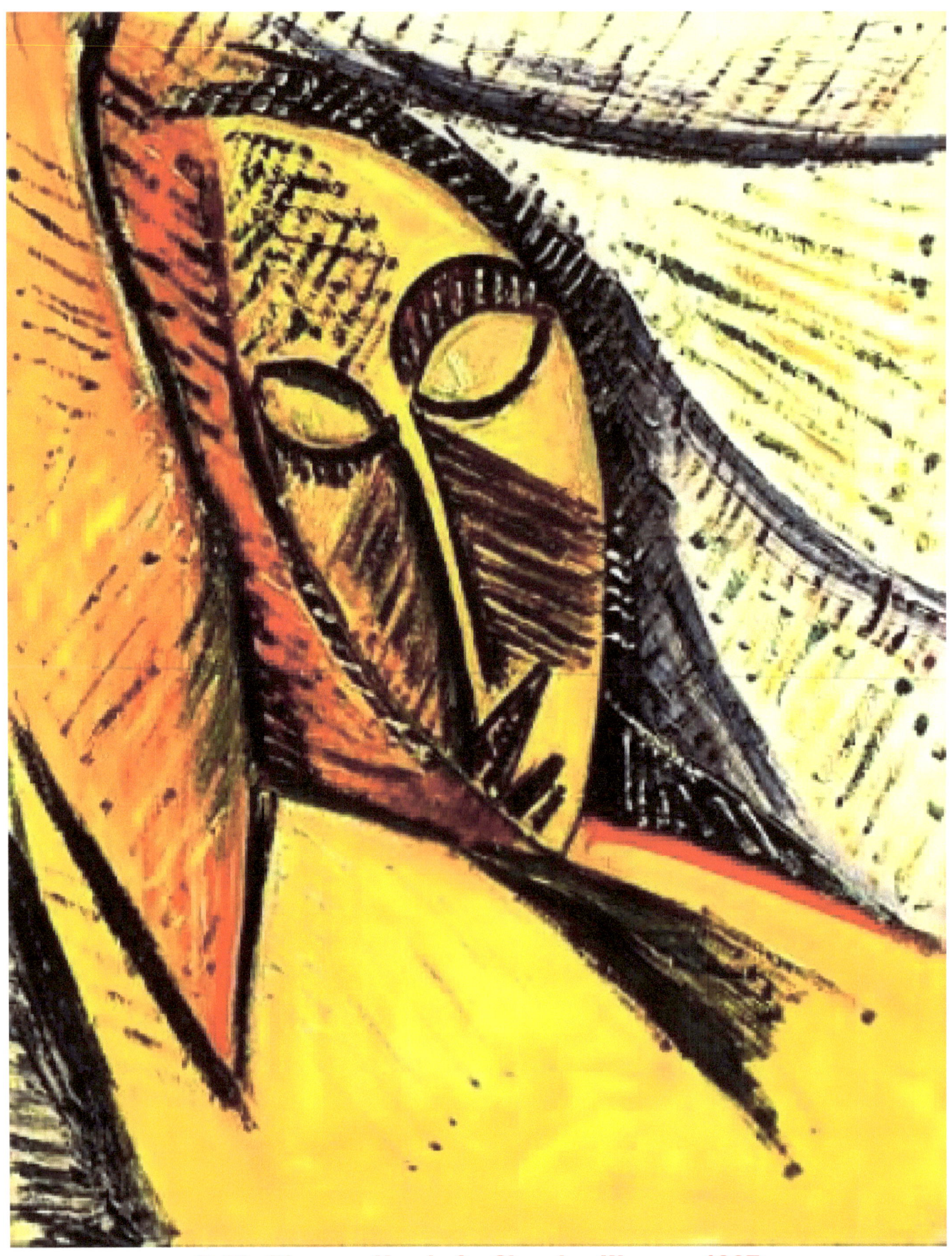

Pablo Picasso, Head of a Sleeping Woman, 1907

Fave Art - 17

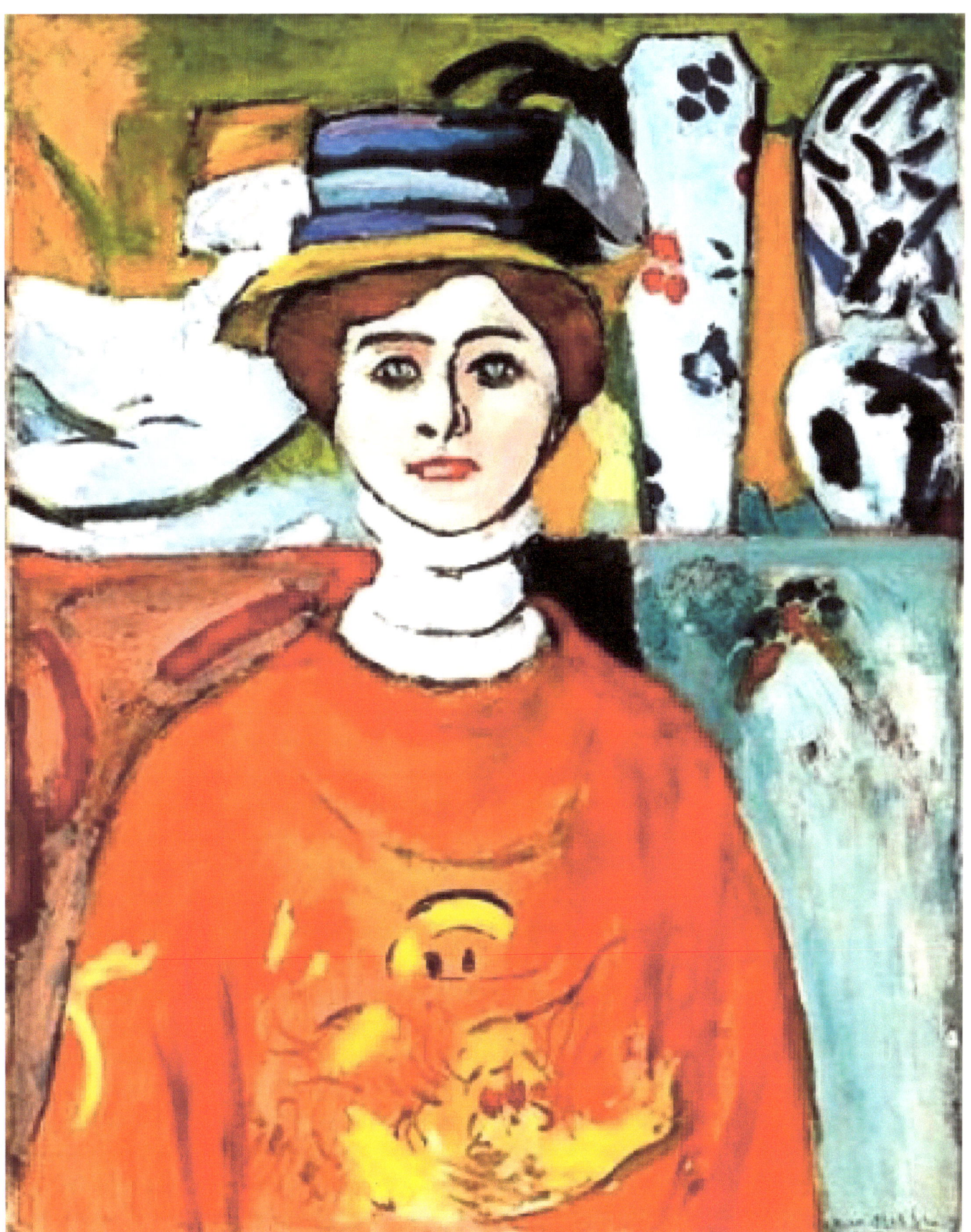

Henri Matisse, The Girl with Green Eyes, 1908

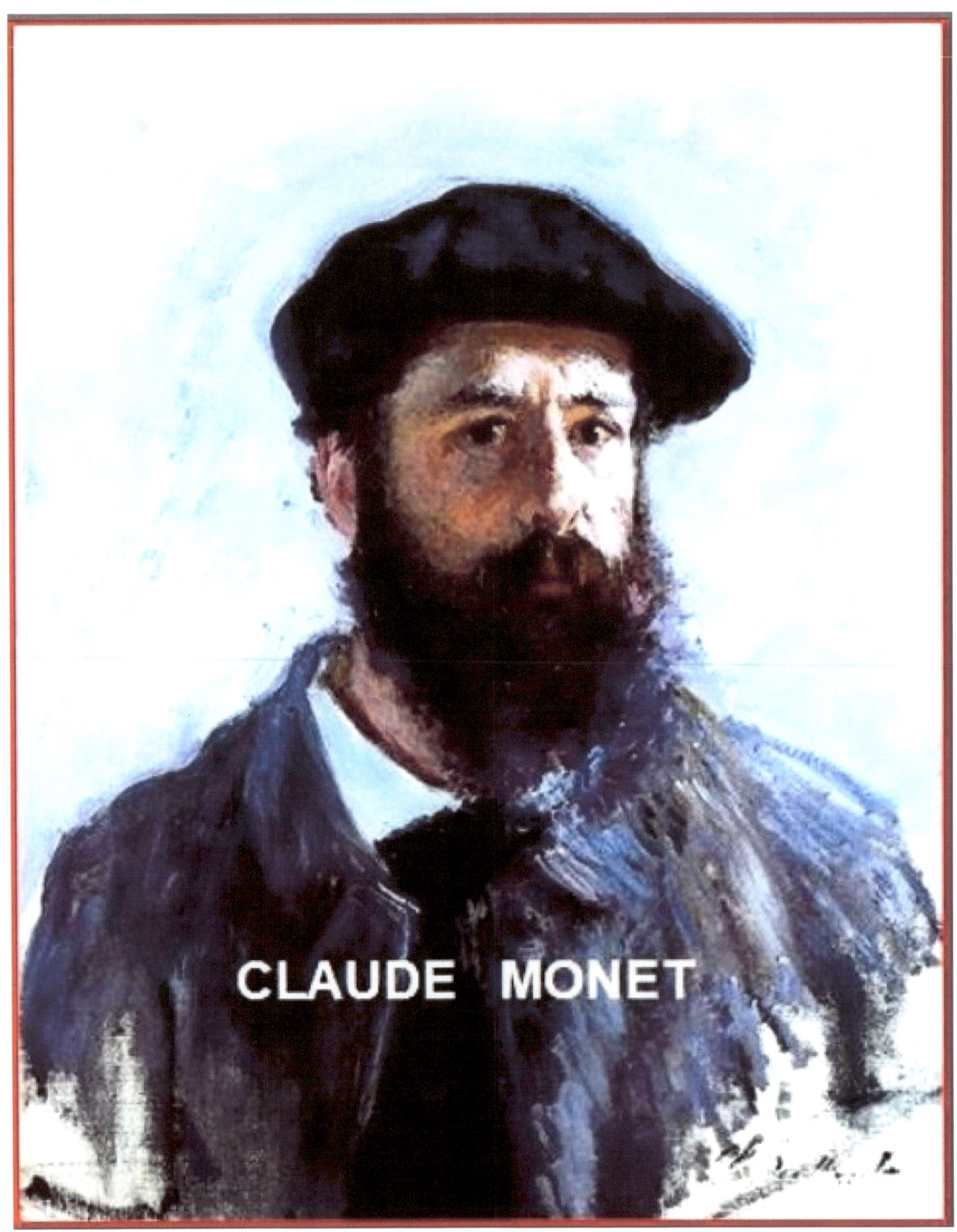

Claude Monet

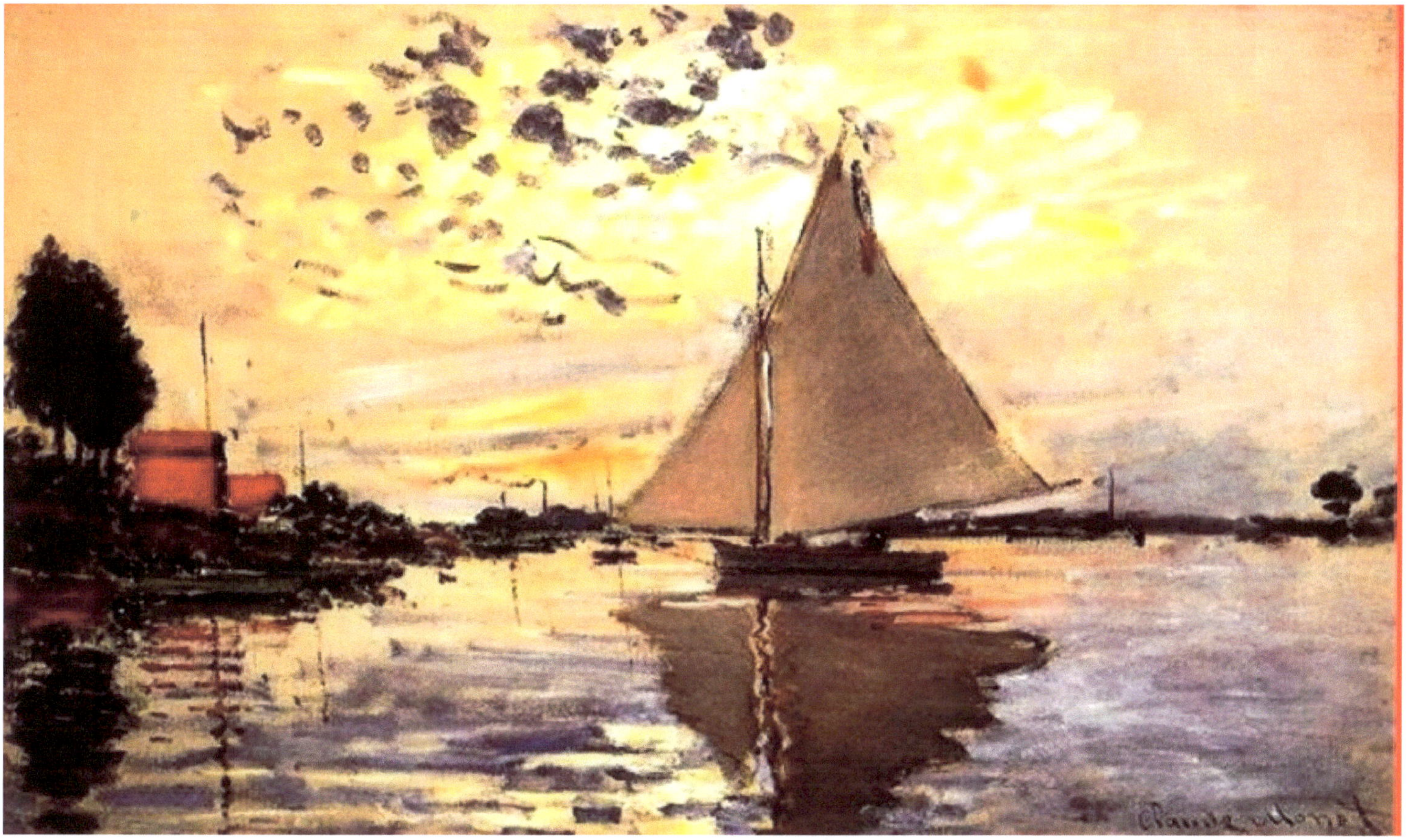

Fave Art - 17

A Claude Monet

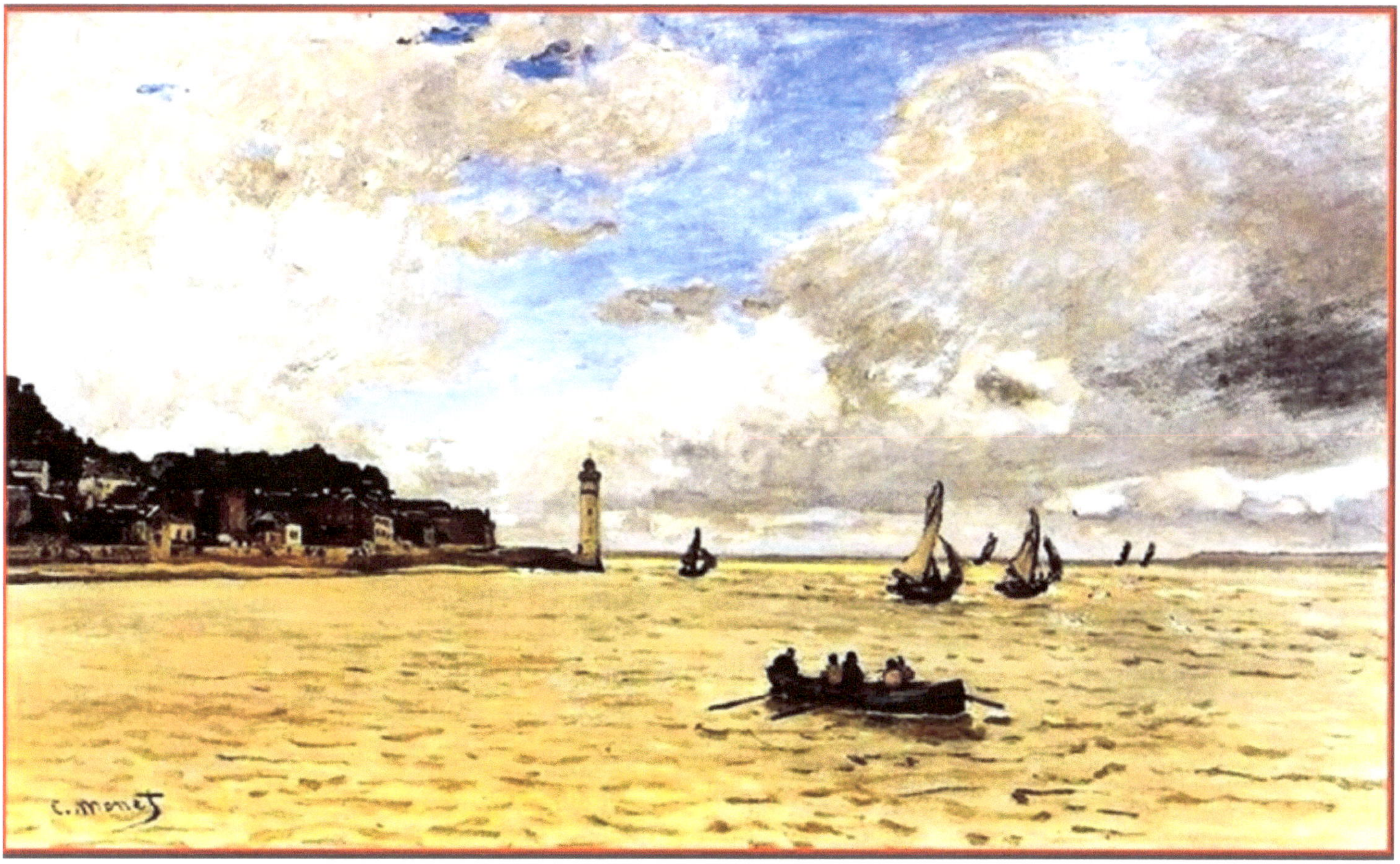

A Claude Monet

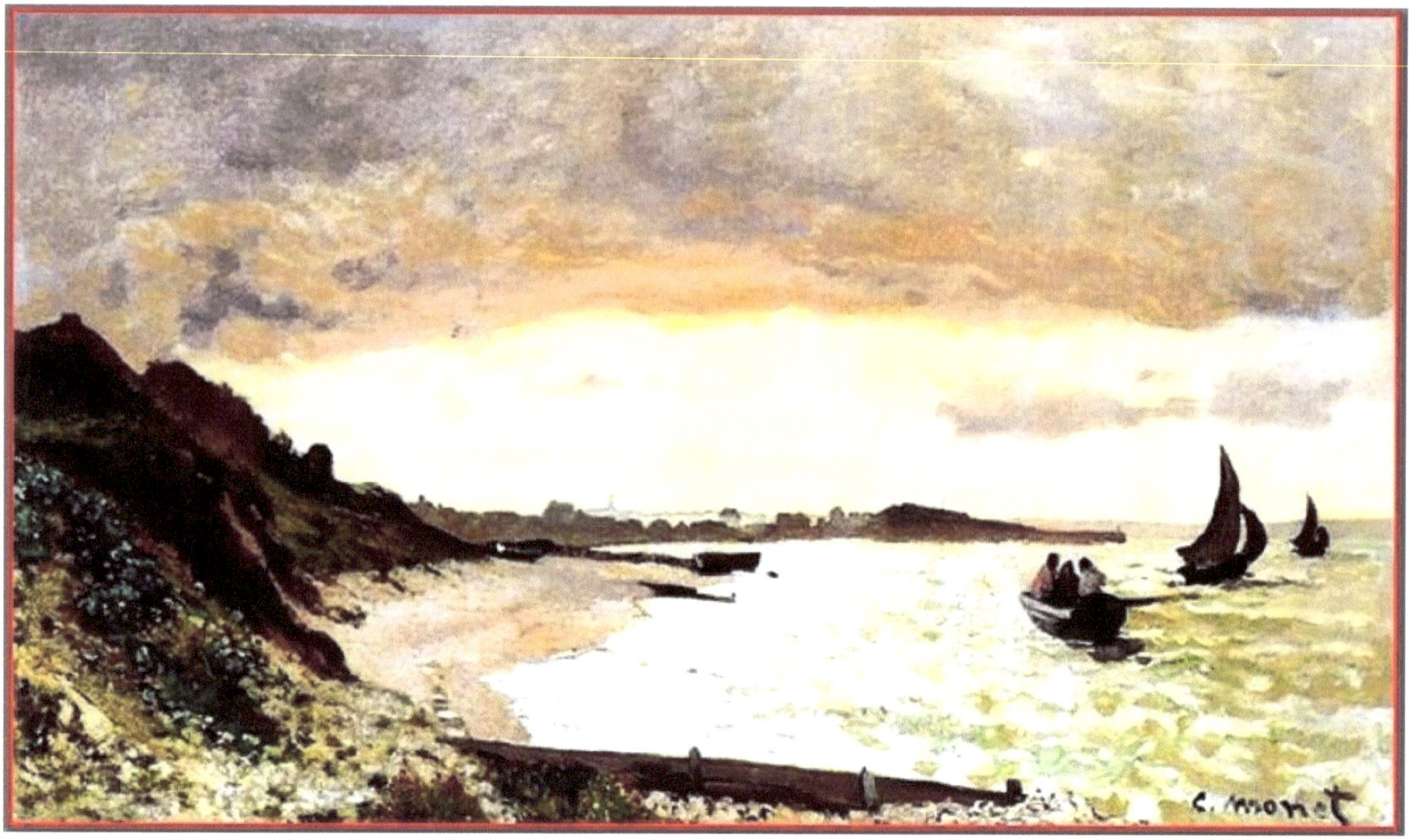

Fave Art - 17

A Claude Monet

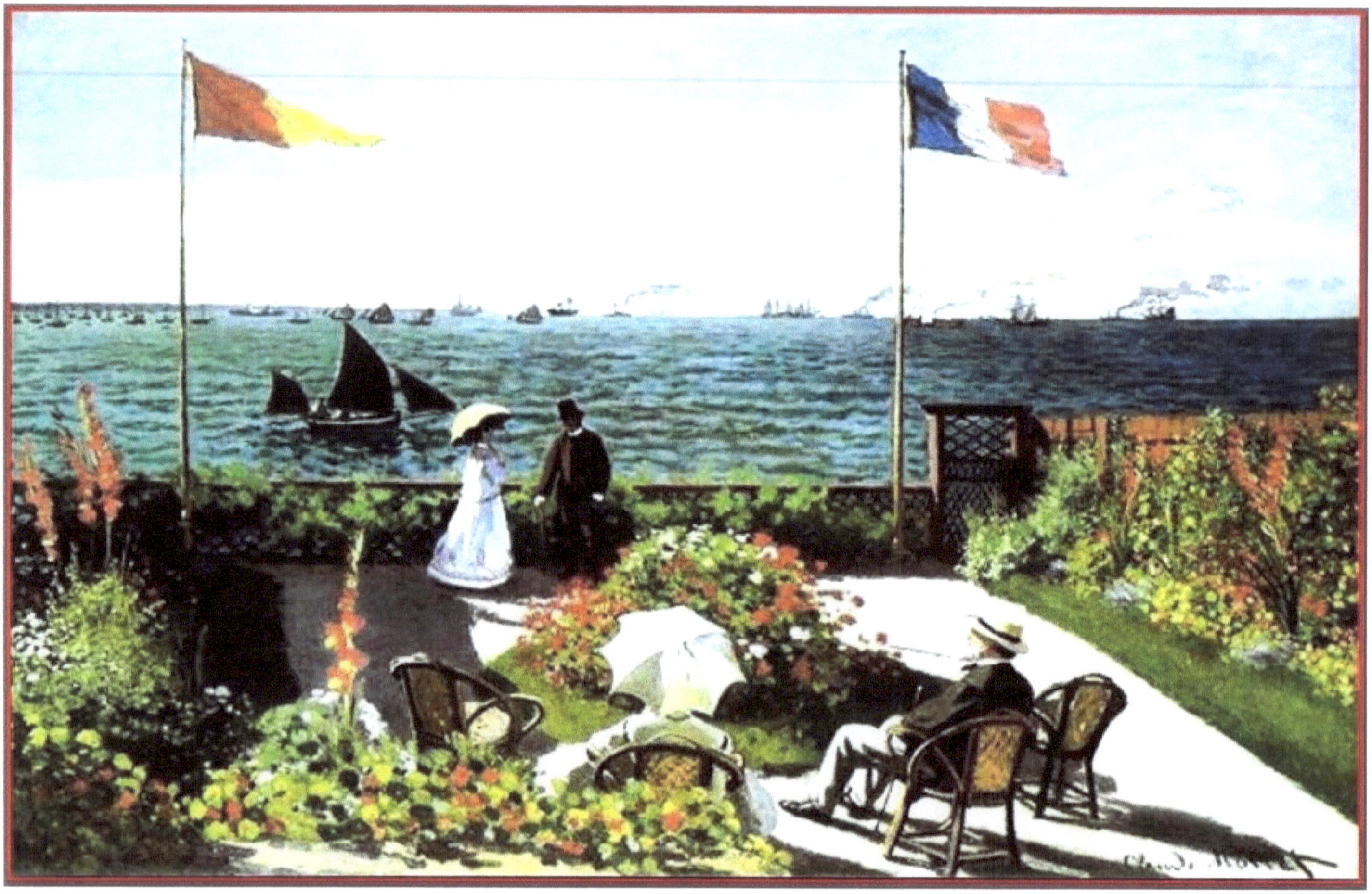

A Claude Monet

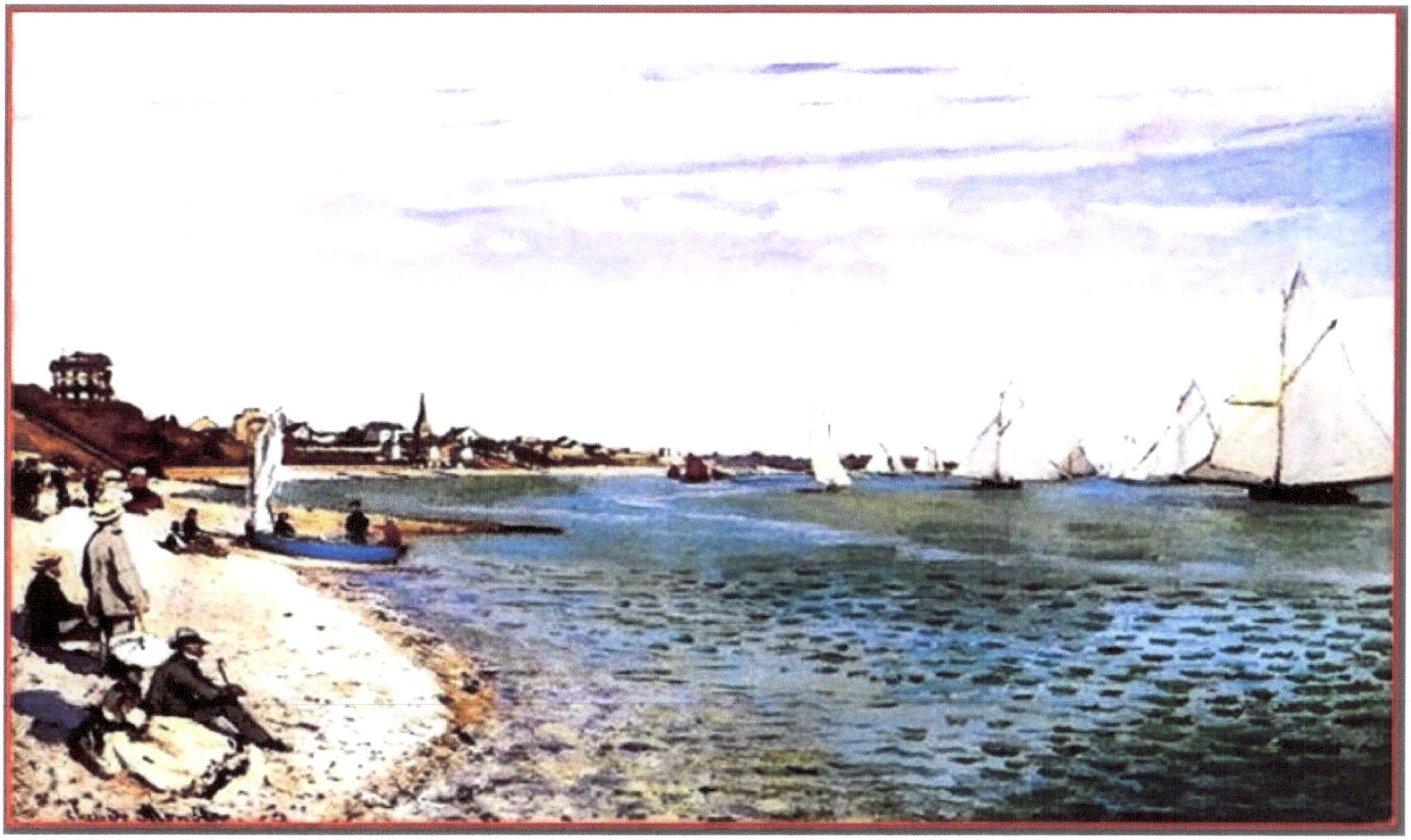

Fave Art - 17

A Claude Monet

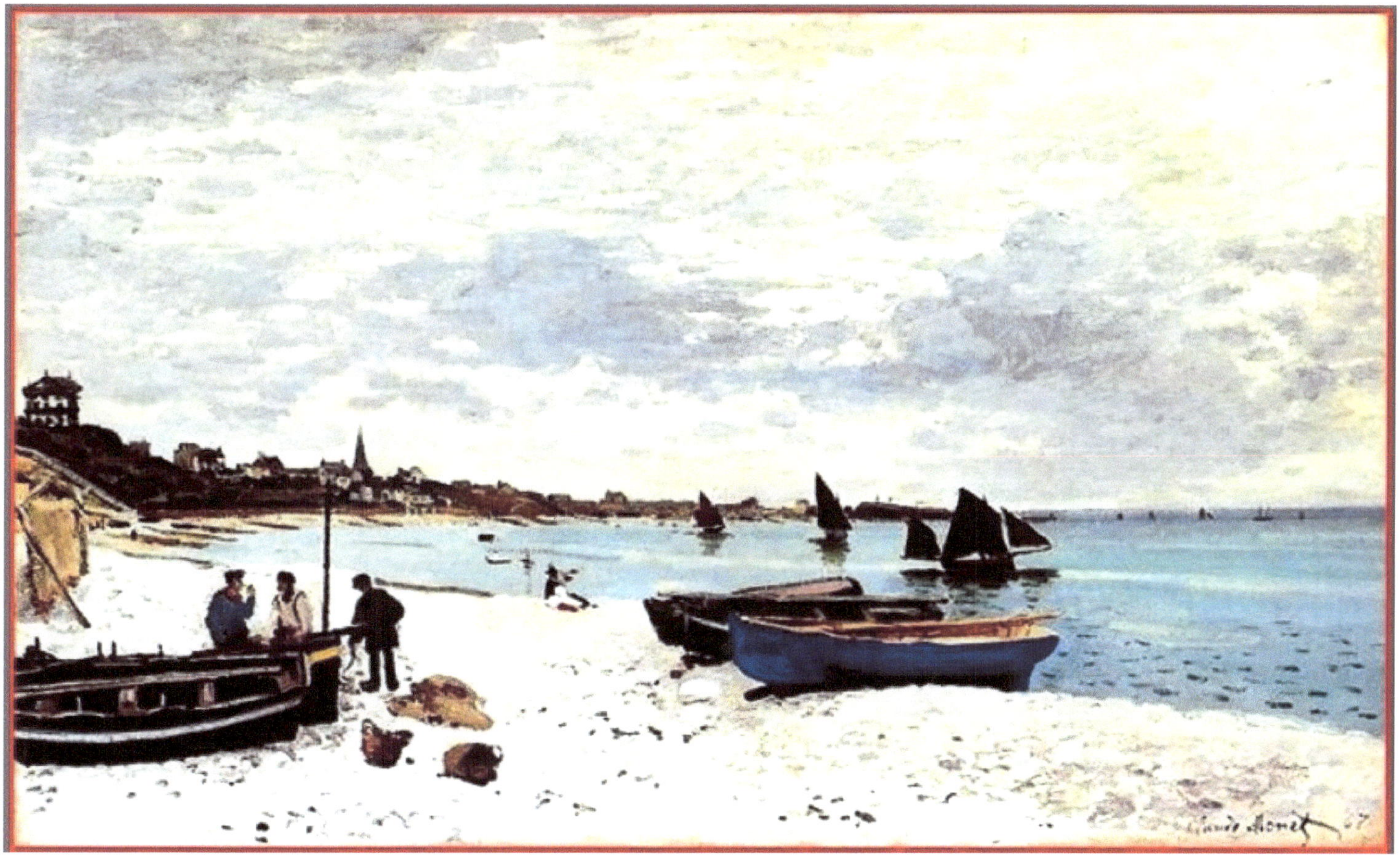

A Claude Monet

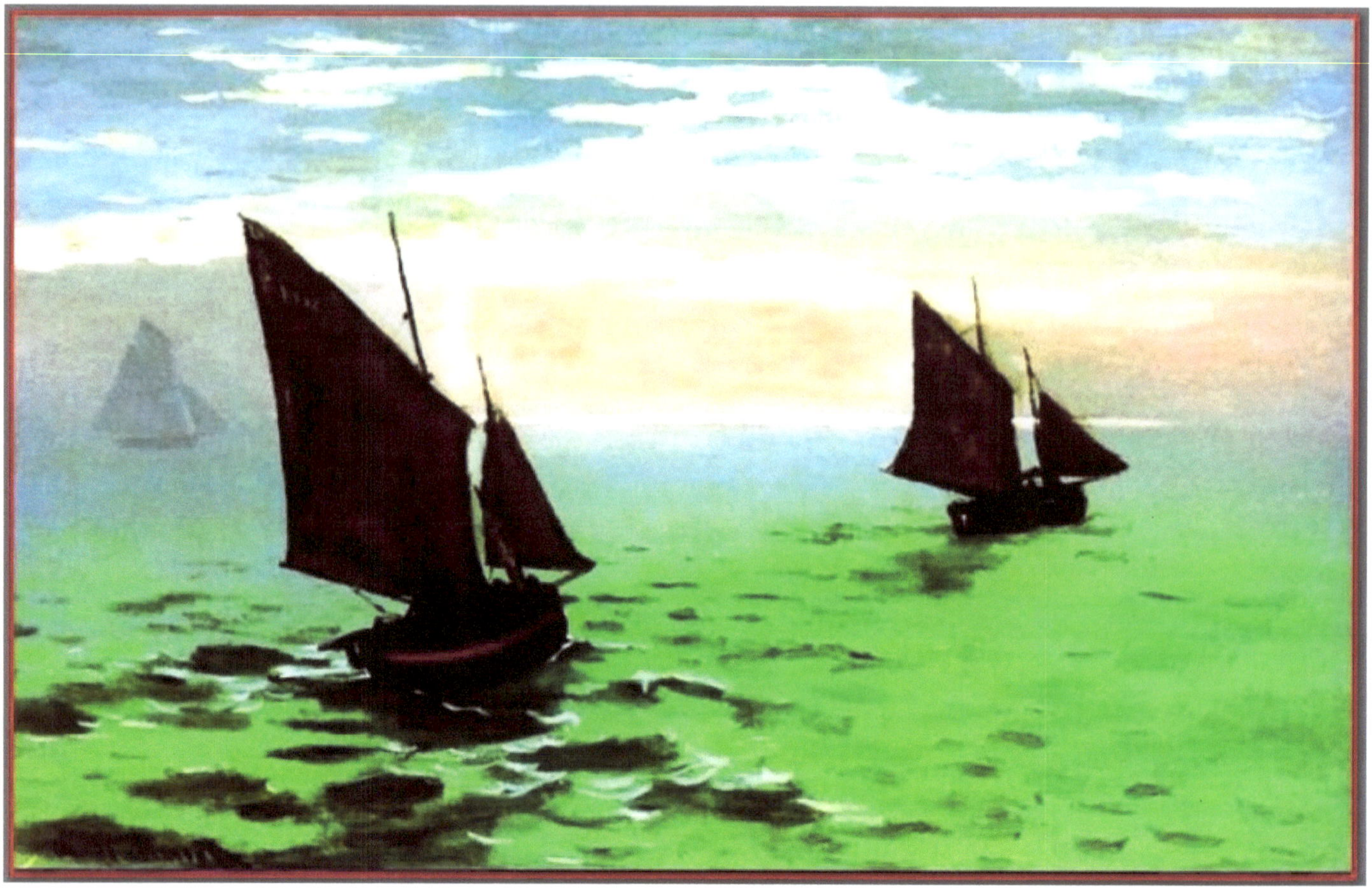

Fave Art - 17

A Claude Monet

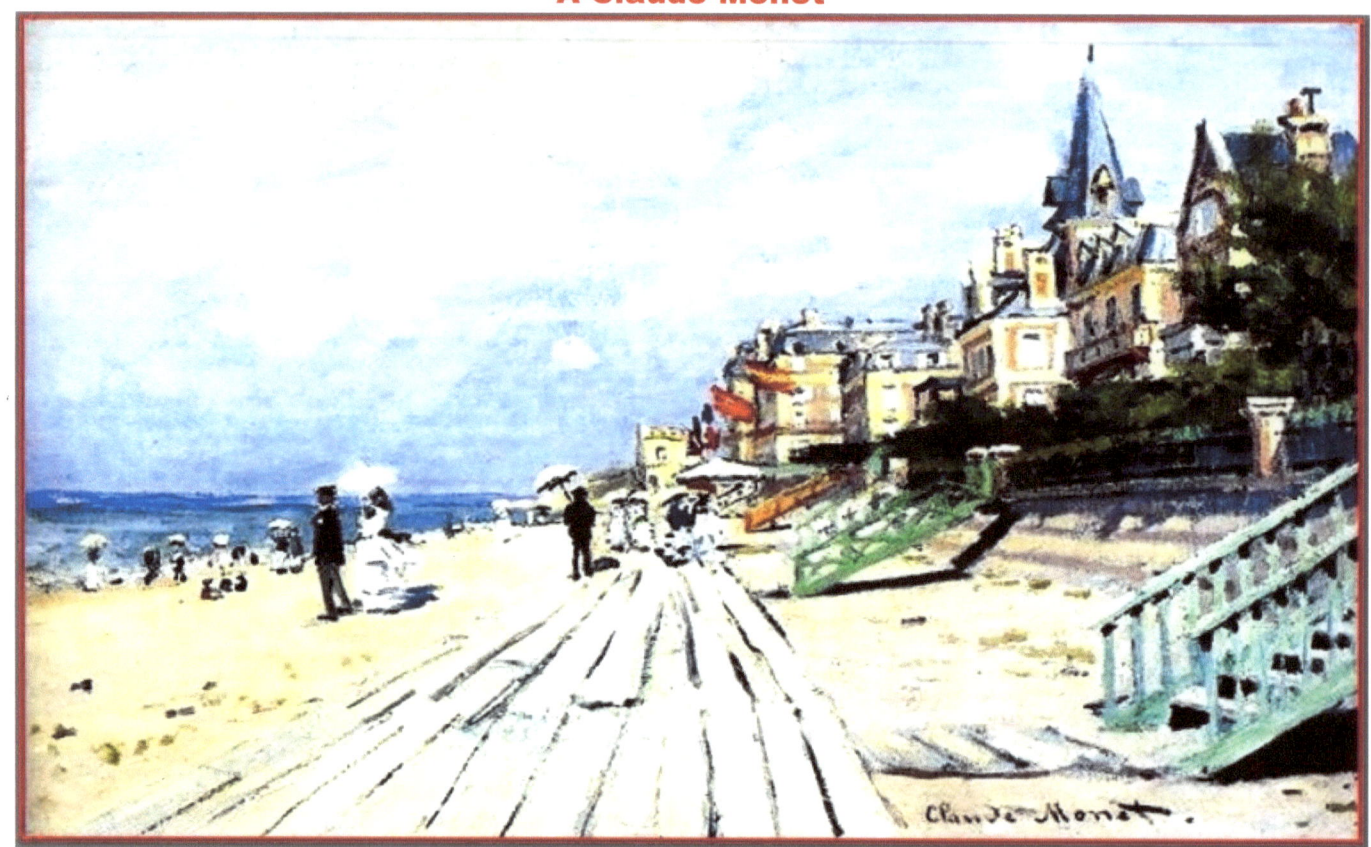

A Claude Monet

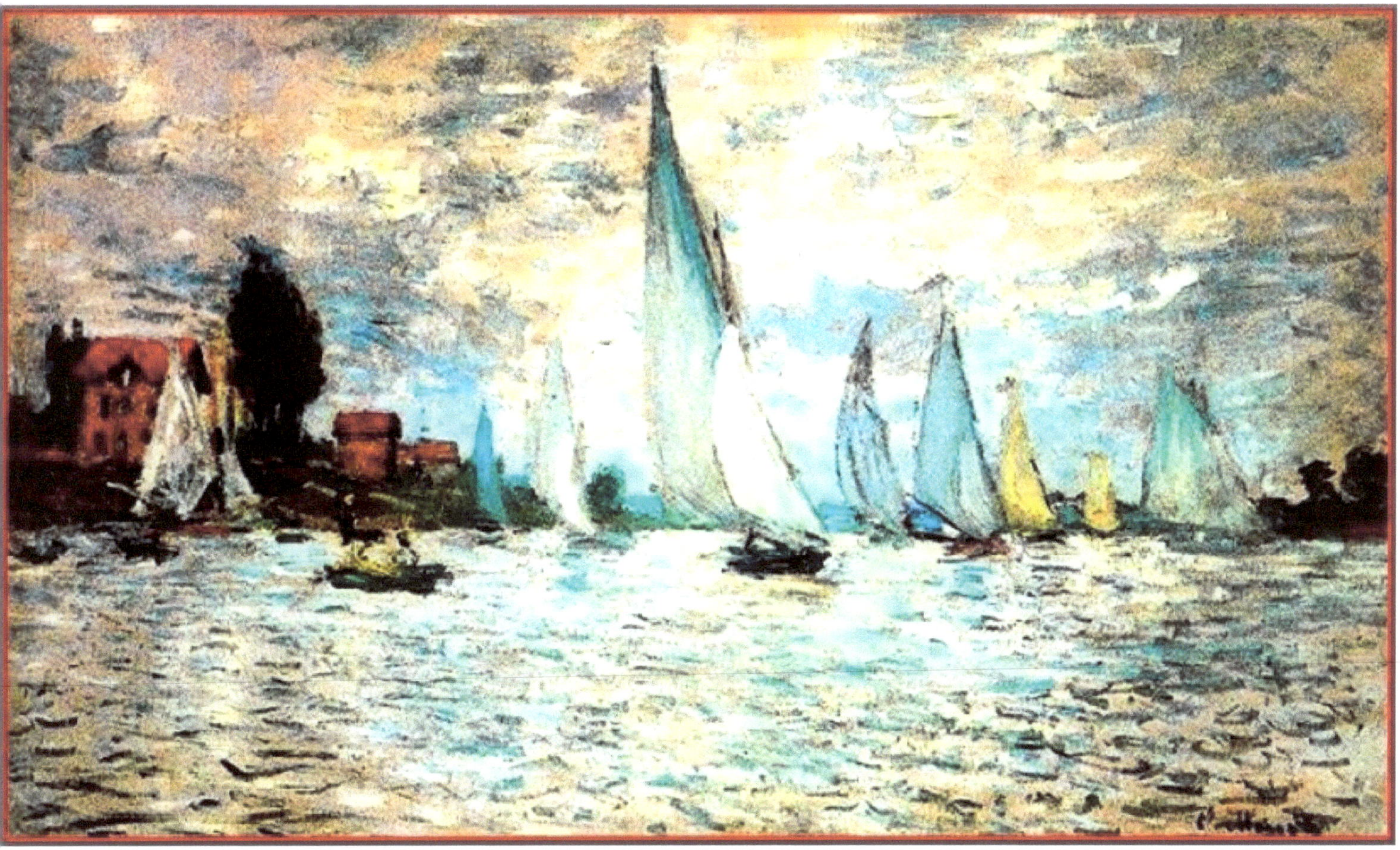

Fave Art - 17

A Claude Monet

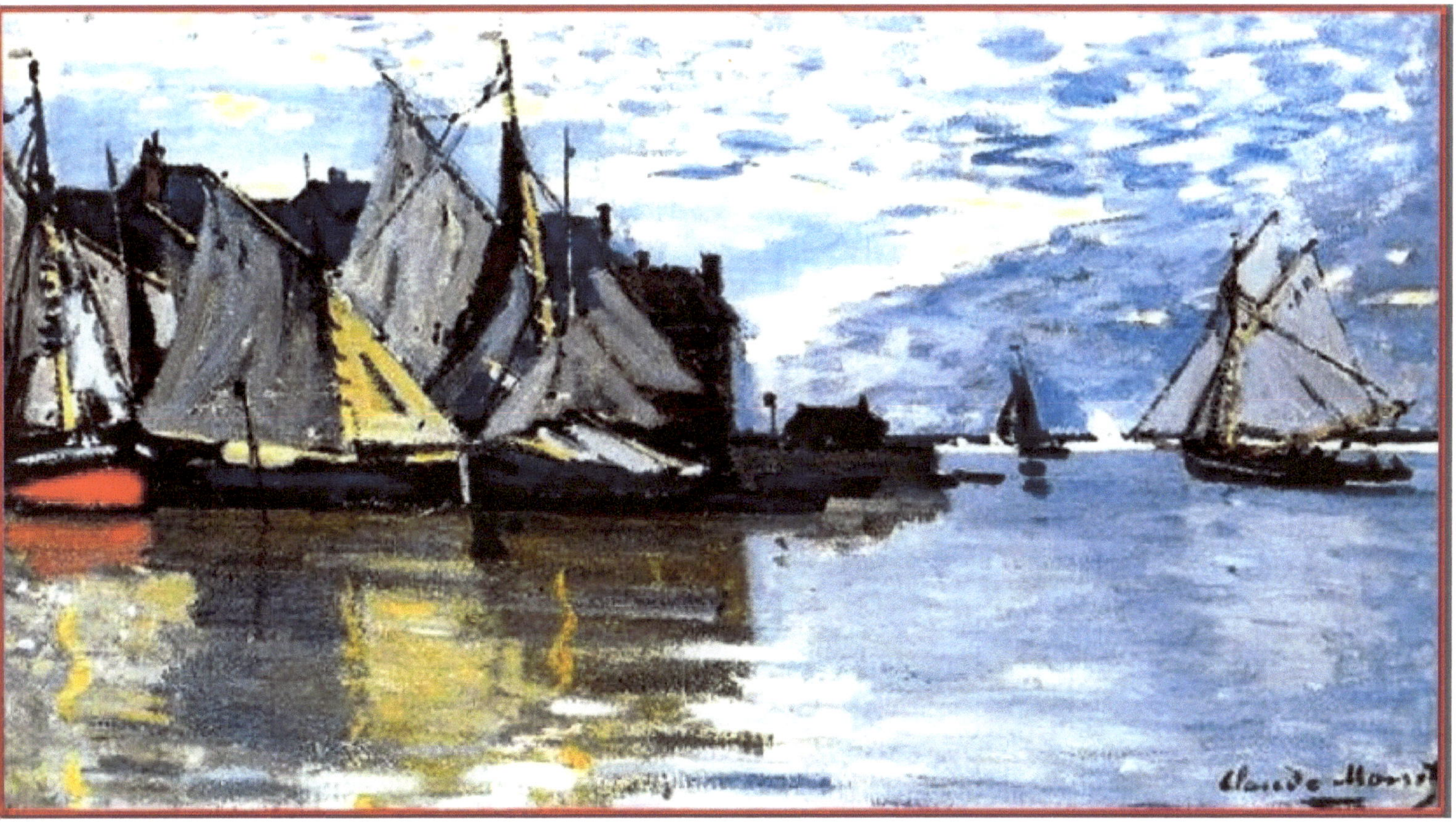

A Claude Monet

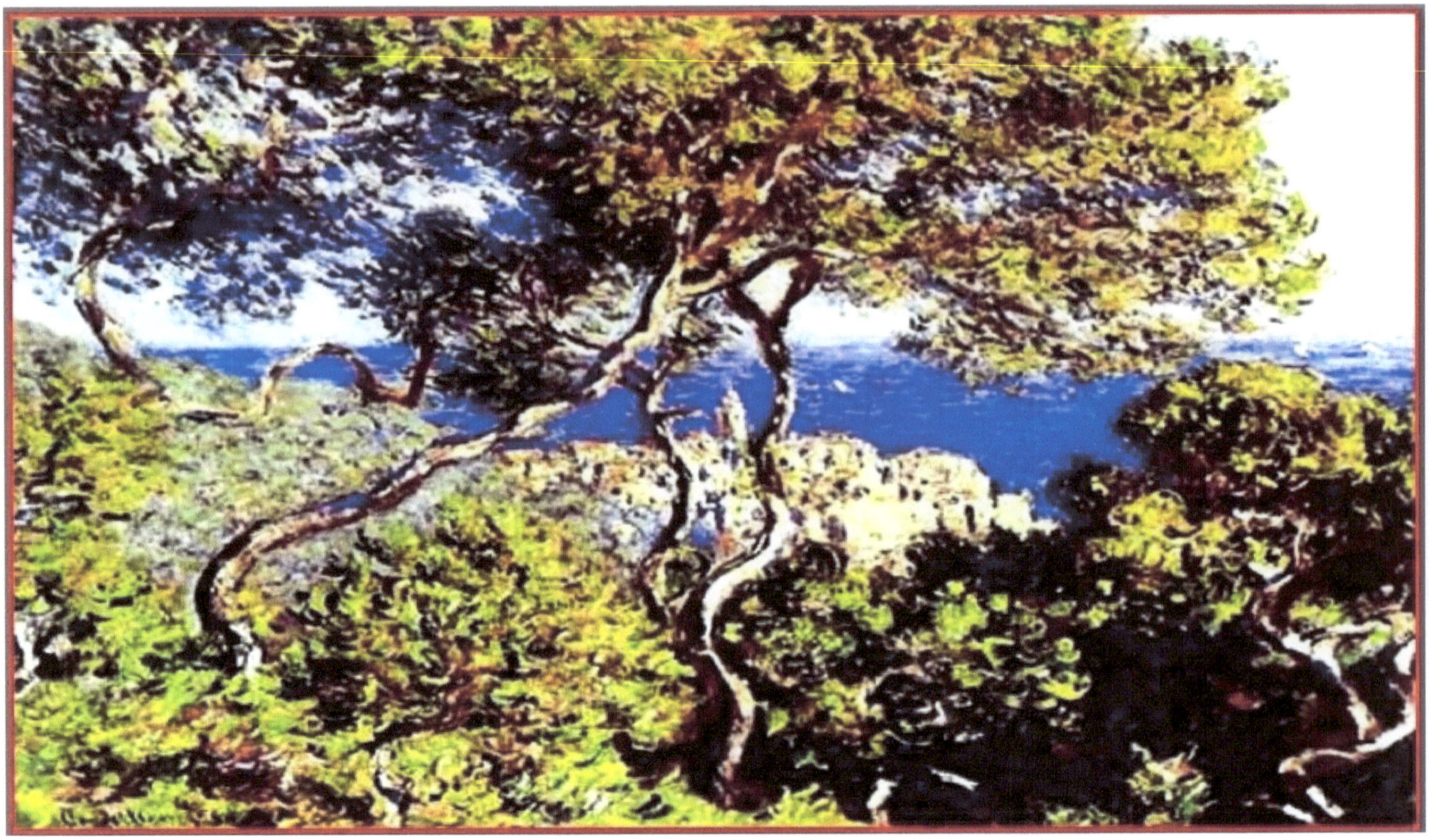

Fave Art - 17

A Claude Monet

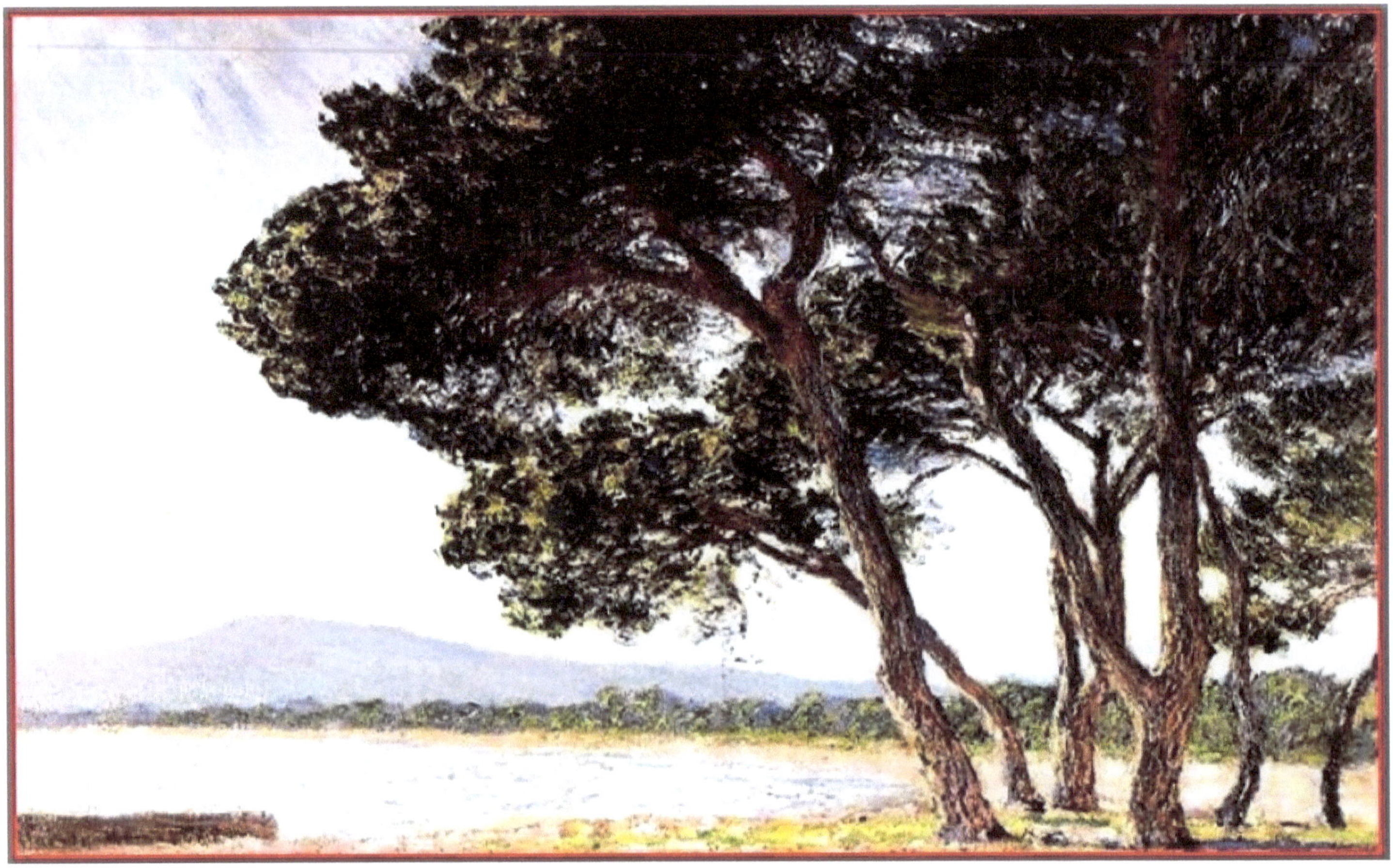

A Claude Monet

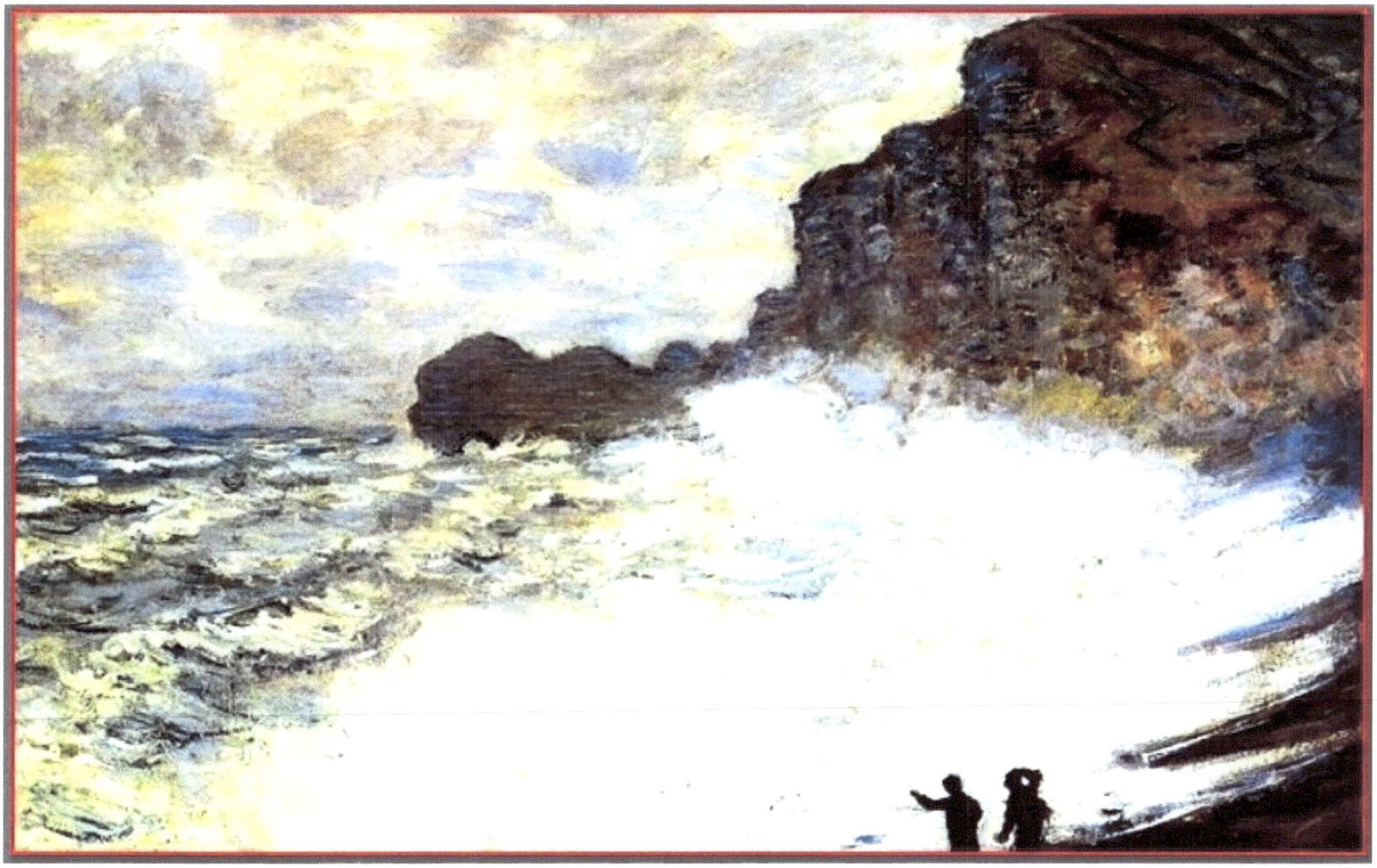

Fave Art - 17

A Claude Monet

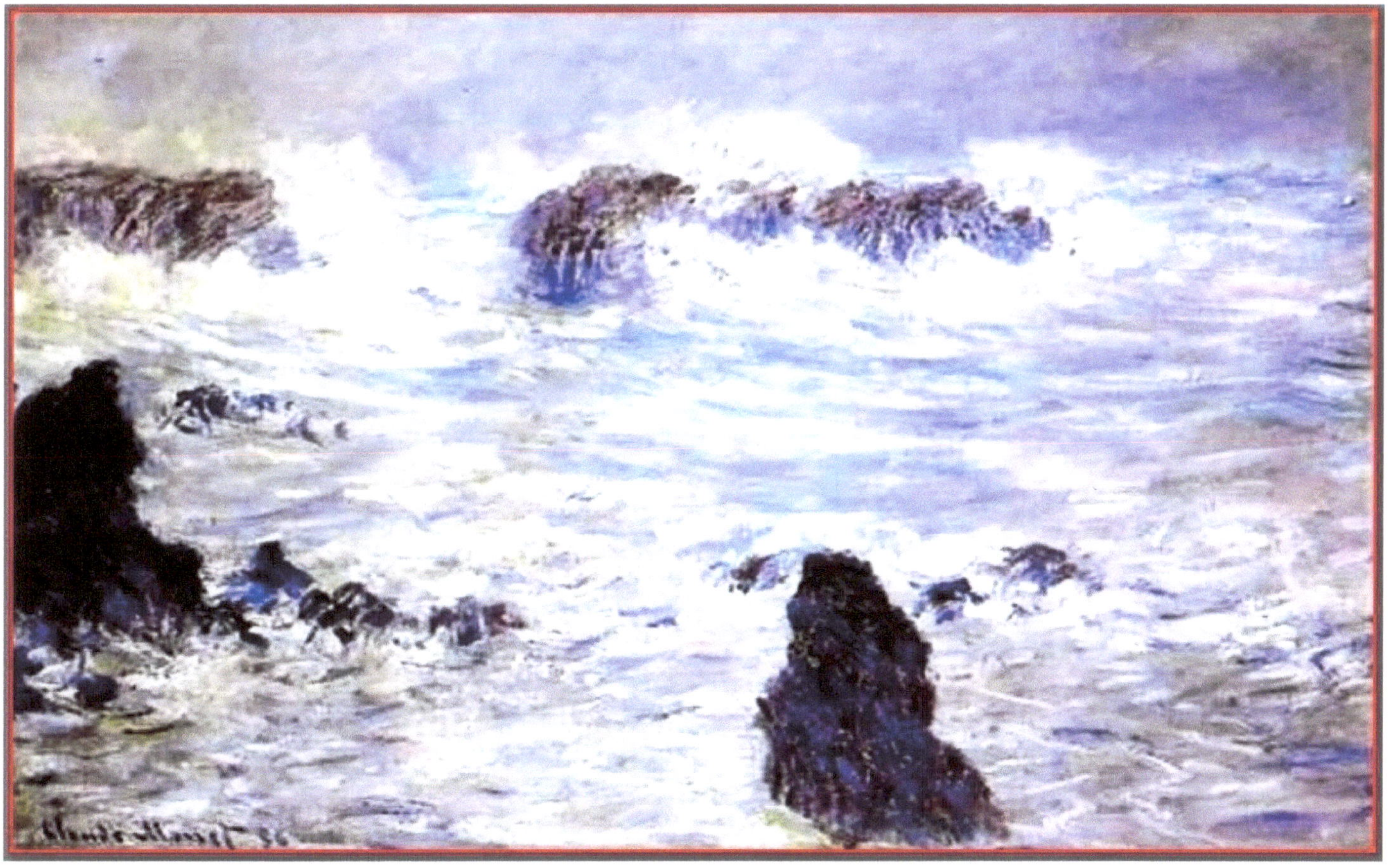

A Claude Monet

Fave Art - 17

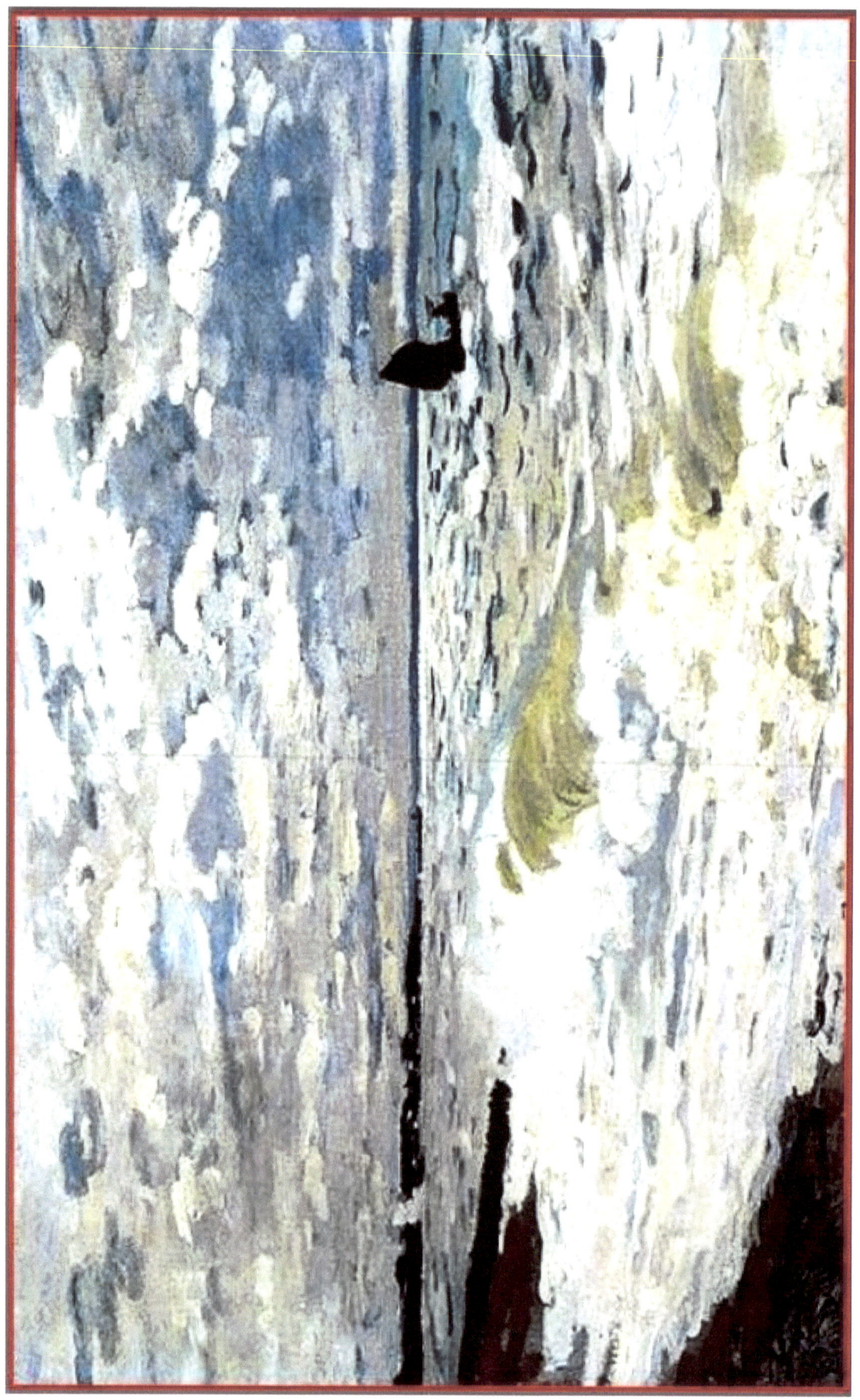

A Claude Monet

Fave Art - 17

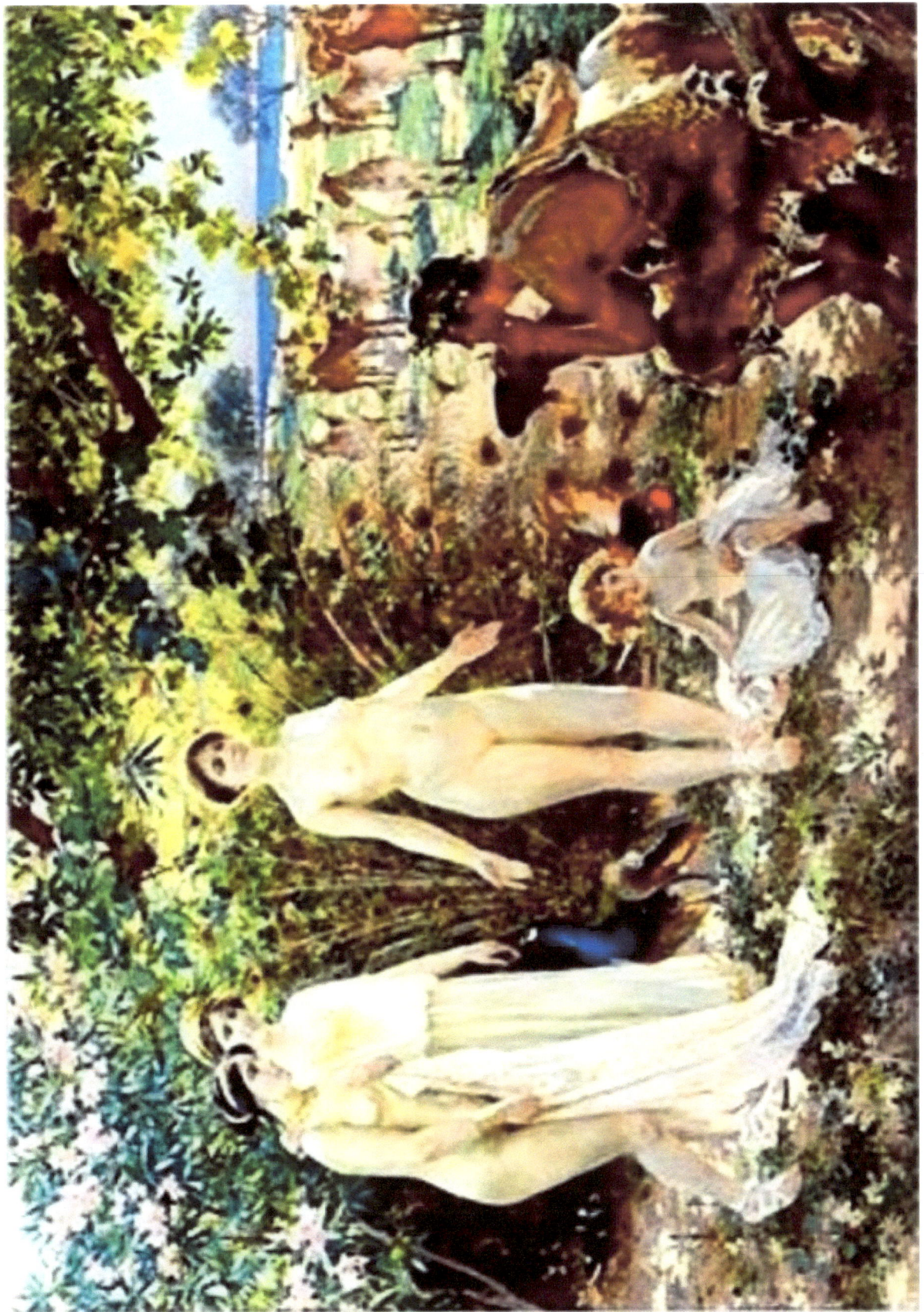

El Juicio de Paris by Enrique Srmonet, c. 1904. This painting depicts Paris judgement. He is inspecting Aphrodite, who is standing naked before him. Hera and Athena watch nearby.

Fave Art - 17

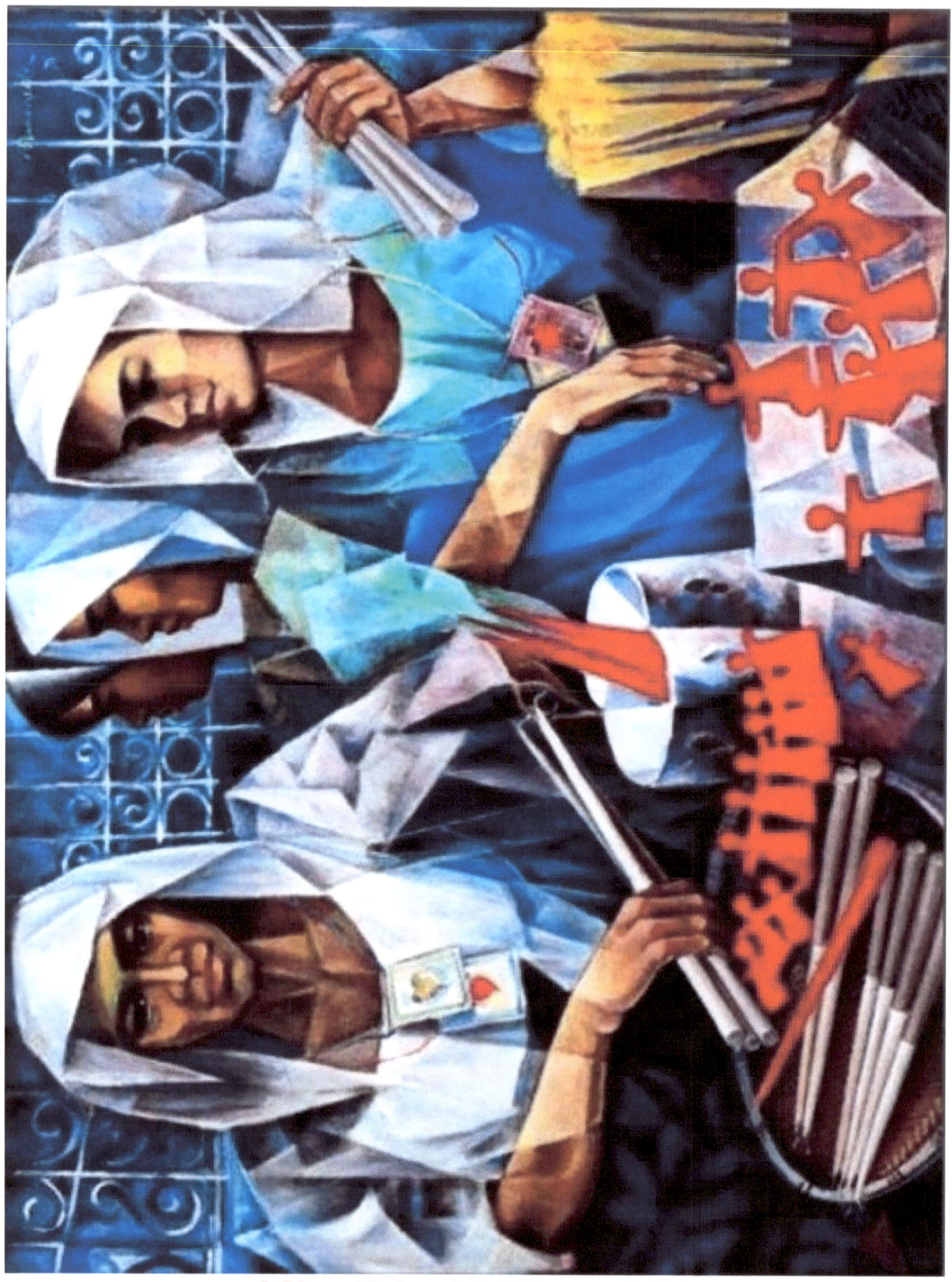

A Pinoy Modern Art, Unknown Artist

Fave Art - 17

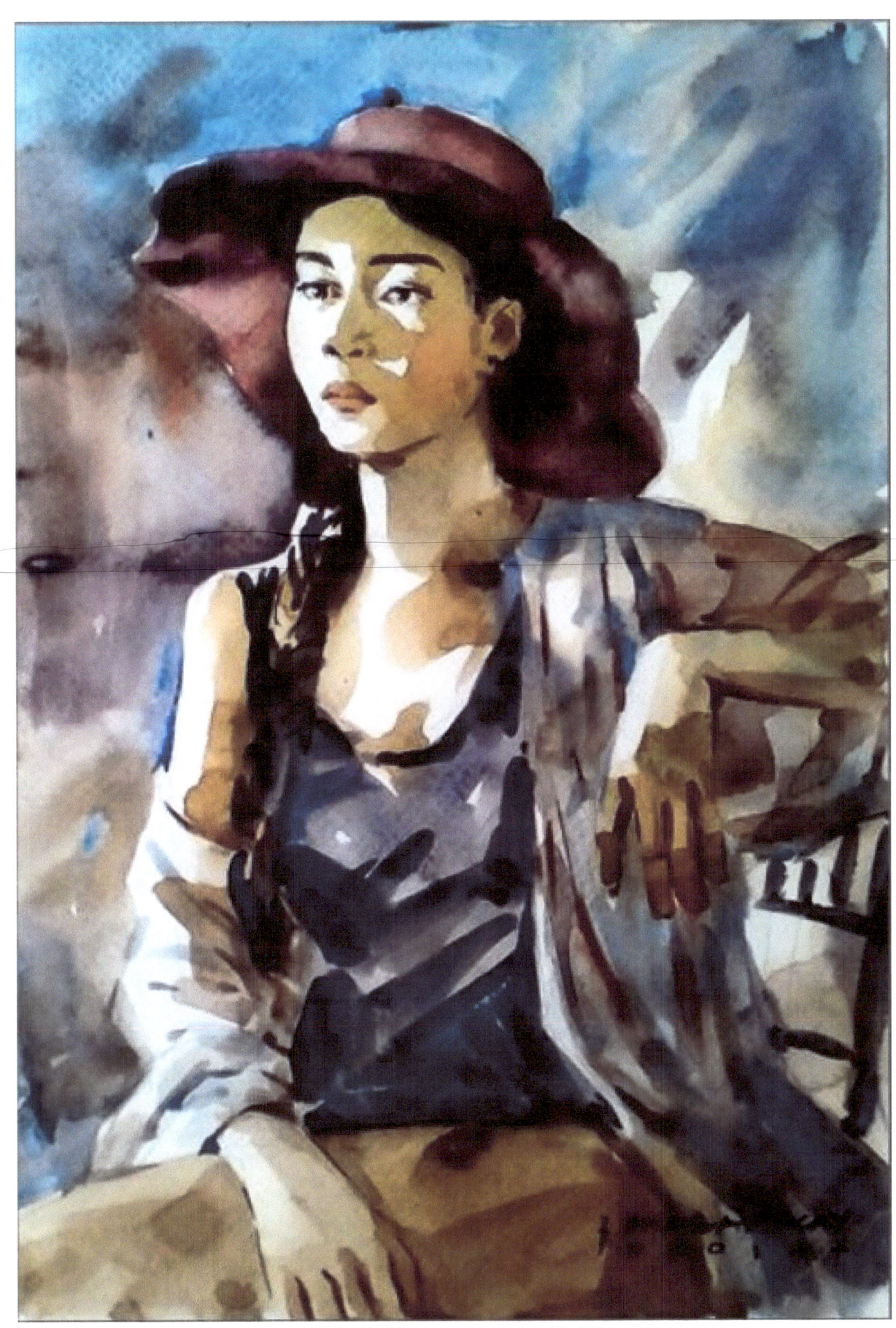

A Nik Masangcay, 2017

Fave Art - 17

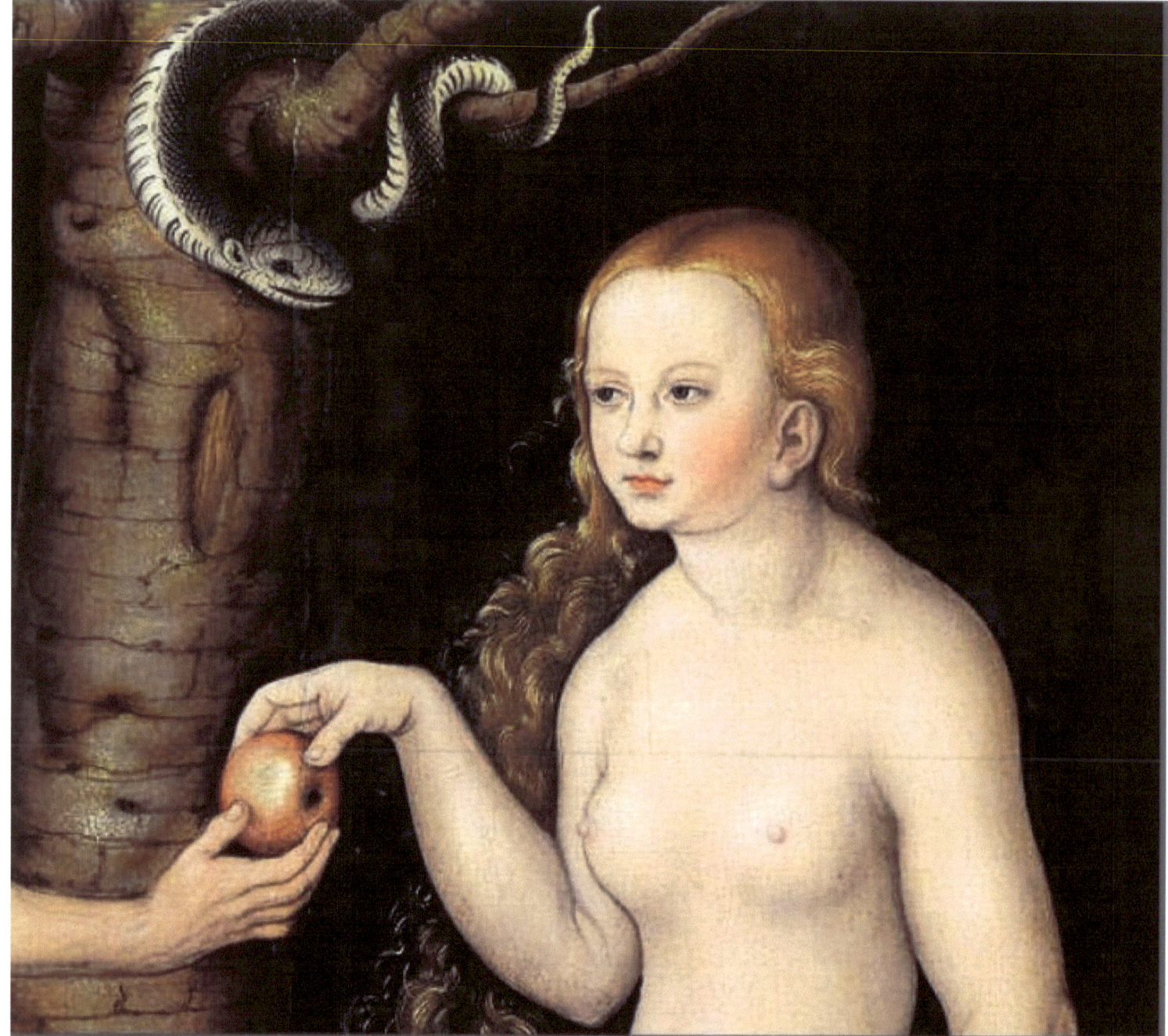

Renaissance Painting, Eve giving apple to Adam

WELCOME! We hope you will enjoy this Fave Art-17 photo album of my favorite random collection of art. Photos are copied from the internet, posters, calendars, cards and art books. You may display this book as coffee table book in your living room, as conversation piece. You may give this as gift. You may cut out each page, 8.5x11 inches, for framing. Printed by Tatay Jobo Elizes under following ISBN Code Numbers:

Fave Art - 17

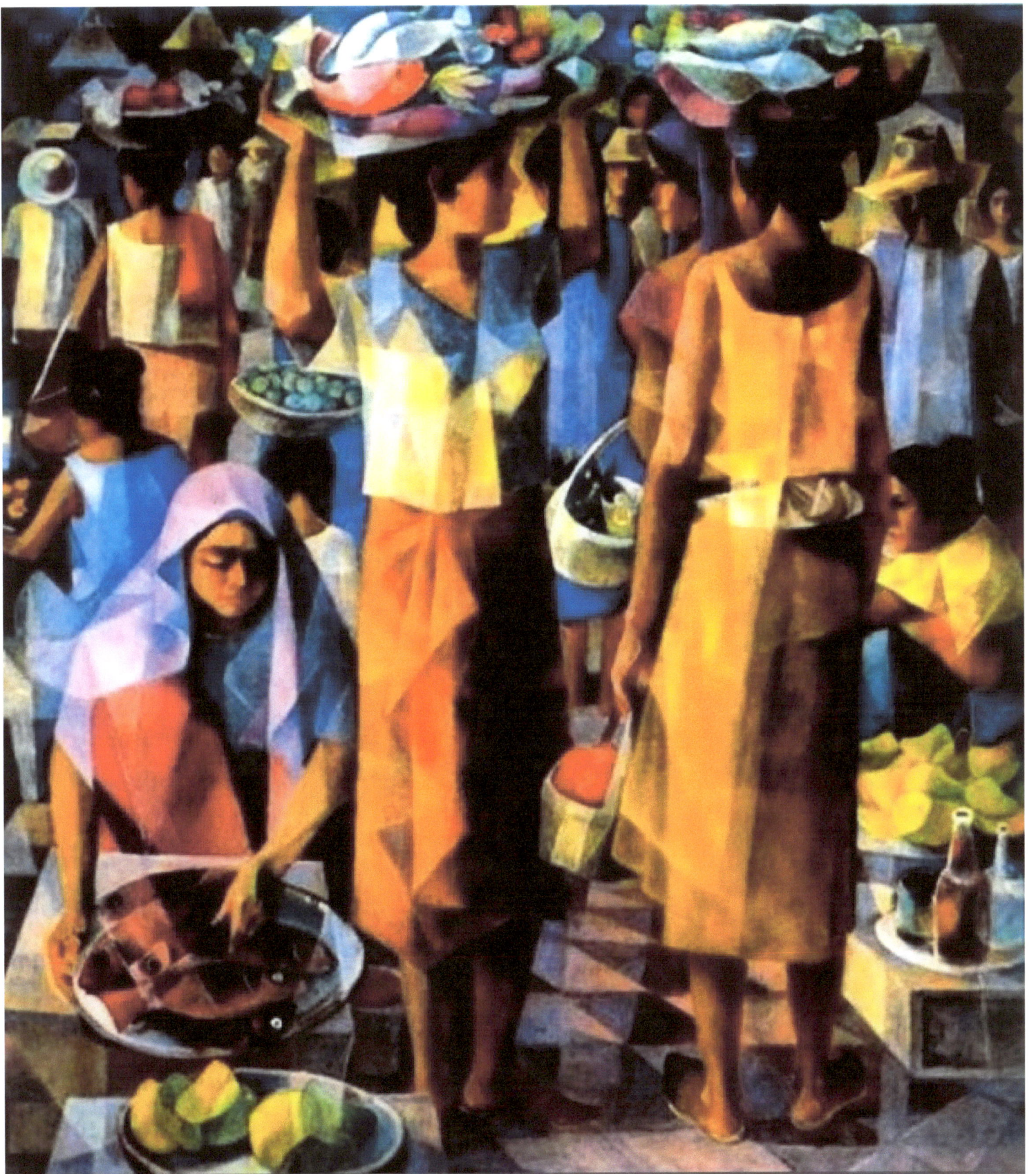

A Modern Pinoy Painting, Artist unknown

Fave Art - 17

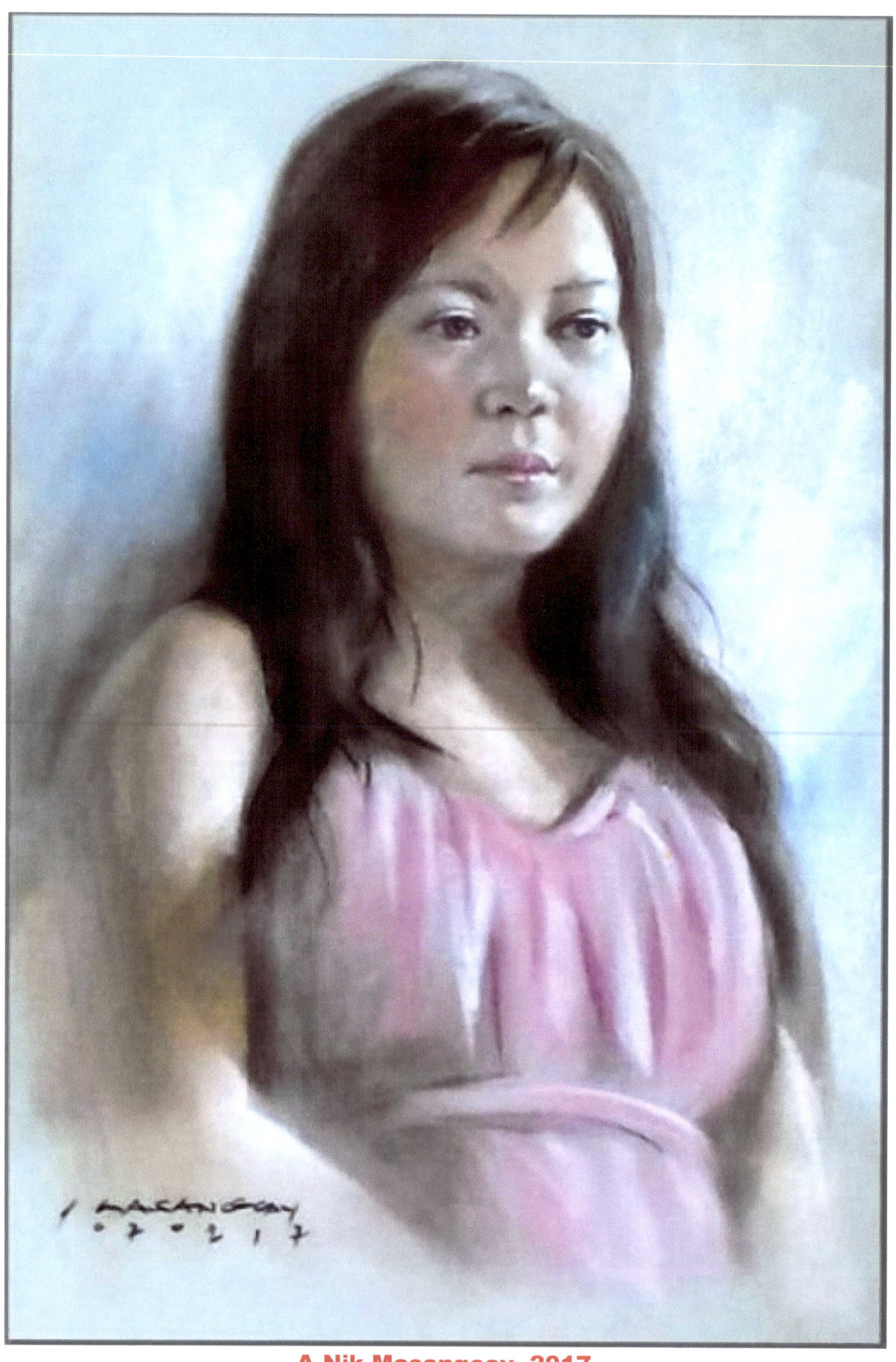

A Nik Masangcay, 2017

www.ingramcontent.com/pod-product-compliance
Lightning Source LLC
Chambersburg PA
CBHW051220220526
45473CB00003B/1116